"Mike is like your trusted advisor, having that conversation with you that you've been dreading but that you know you need to have. At the end, your future will be a lot brighter, because you'll be heading into the light."

—Chris Bolinger,
Amazon best-selling author of *Daily Strength for Men*

"Most men are isolated, self-sufficient, independent, macho, and living in the darkness. Mike Hatch gives a biblical foundation and argument for living radically and powerfully in the light. Mike's life proves it works!"

—Dr. Hal Hadden,
Founder of Christian Leadership Concepts

"Mike Hatch takes men on an empowering journey by sharing his journey, insights from Scripture, winsome stories, and a simple rubric for understanding how to root one's identity in Jesus Christ."

—Dr. Kurt Bjorklund,
Author of *Prayers for Today*; Senior Pastor,
Orchard Hill Church, Wexford, Pennsylvania

"This book is for every man…young or old! Mike deliberately takes you on a journey using his life and the lives of men in the Bible to uncover genuine manhood: To be known by God, grown by God, owned by God, and empowered by God. He exposes the starvation we endure without the permanent indwelling of the Holy Spirit. His transparency inspires you and his passion compels you to go ALL-IN with the God who created you."

—J.S. Shelton,
Author of *UNMUZZLED:
Escaping Sexual Sin, Satan's Grip on Men*

"As a ministry brother, I've had a behind-the-scenes look at Mike's life and share in his passion to empower men with the Gospel. With vulnerability and 20+ years of pastoral experience, he wrote this book to help guys like you and me stop hiding in the darkness of past mistakes by stepping into the light of God's grace. I'll be sharing this one with my guys!"

—Kent Chevalier,
Athletes in Action: Pittsburgh Steelers Chaplain,
Pittsburgh, Pennsylvania

T0001393

"I am hard-pressed to name any men's book with more searing honesty, courage, and truth—the truth that will set you free—than my friend Mike Hatch's *Manhood: Empowered by the Light of the Gospel*. Mike offers a realistic and powerful path to freedom on the masculine journey. In my 10 years in men's ministry, I have found that men are uncomfortable admitting the obvious, that they can't meet all their own needs, that they are not self-sufficient. Like the angel finding Gideon cowering in the winepress, Mike names the inadequate mess of masculinity a mighty warrior and calls forth the redeemed man of God within us. He invites us to leave the shadowy darkness and walk forth into Christ's glorious light."

—Bob Jamison

"Mike understands the deep insecurity many men experience but desperately work to conceal. Through his own story and years serving men of all ages, Mike will help you recognize insecurity as a symptom of your disempowerment. You are not who you could be, and deep down you know it. Through scripture, encouragement, and transparency, Mike will lead you to a better empowered form of manhood. And, right now, the world needs men empowered by God, empowered to serve, sacrifice, and submit to Him."

—Chase Replogle,
Pastor and Author

"As I read *Manhood: Empowered by the Light of the Gospel*, I was struck by the authenticity of the message and the messenger. This is a resource that highlights the strength of character every man desires, a depth of manhood grounded in honesty, self-awareness, and God-ordained servanthood. I recommend Mike Hatch, his ministry to men, and this work without hesitation."

—Dr. Craig Fry,
President of CLC

"Mike asks the questions: Are tired of hiding? Are you worn out from carrying the burden of shame and guilt? Is the dissonance between who you really are and who people think you are tearing you apart? I believe that we all deal with those issues at some point in life. Mike does a great job sharing his journey to empowerment and wholeness in a raw and compelling manner. His words will encourage you to refuse to remain in the darkness and challenge you to step into the light."

—Chris Buda,
Attorney, Pastor and Executive Director
of the Pittsburgh Experiment

MANHOOD: EMPOWERED

by the Light of the Gospel

BY

MIKE HATCH

TABLE OF CONTENTS

ACKNOWLEDGMENTS

To my beautiful bride, Lisa. Thank you for being my faithful advocate and my brick wall of truth. This book simply doesn't exist without God's grace manifest through you.

To my son, Matteo. May this book serve as a reminder that your heavenly Father will never leave you nor forsake you.

INTRODUCTION

When I was in college, I worked at the Tie Rack in the Pittsburgh International Airport Airmall selling neck ties. One evening I had just finished my lunch and was in the bathroom rinsing the used Tupperware container when a guy in the stall behind me came to my attention. I thought it was peculiar that, when he came out of the stall, he raced out of the restroom without washing his hands.

Then, at about that moment, I heard something strange from the other side of the restroom. As I peered around the wall of sinks to investigate, I saw three women cackling, whispering to each other, and looking over at me!

Now, my first thought was, "Wow, how embarrassing, those women are in the men's restroom." Then, as the truth of the situation sunk in, I realized, "No, I'm in the women's restroom!"

No wonder that "guy" in the stall behind me left so quickly. "He" was a woman.

I felt my face get flush with warmth. Then a feeling of paralysis gripped my whole body as I stood staring at myself in the mirror. I had to do something quick. But what? How was I going to save face? How could I avoid being found out by a broader audience? How was I going to get out of this alive—and with my dignity intact?

I made the only acceptable decision I could think of: I decided to walk out of that restroom like I owned the place—like I had as much right to be there as anyone else. As I walked out of the women's restroom that day, head held high, several women walked right by me on their way in and never looked twice at me. Whew! I lived to see another day!

My reason for telling you this story is that most of my young life was spent feeling like that day in the women's restroom—particularly the part where I was paralyzed from fear, feeling caught in a place I shouldn't be, and trying to find a way out without being noticed. I was living in the dark, engaging in secret sins I had worked hard at keeping secret. I felt like I could never be my authentic self, because no one would want to be around that guy.

A deep sense of insecurity characterized my life, and I lived out of fear that one day someone would find out the awful truth about my sin, and then the masquerade would be over. I thought my only recourse was to fake it and pretend like I owned the place. Feigning confidence became my go-to coping mechanism to hide my insecurity.

What I didn't realize was that this impostor syndrome I was struggling with was a symptom of a deeper, more fundamental problem of living in the dark. Jesus said in John 3:19–20, "This is the verdict: Light has come into the world, but people loved darkness instead of light because their deeds were evil. Everyone who does evil hates the light, and will not come into the light for fear that their deeds will be exposed."

To live in the dark was disempowering because I was denying the truth about who I was, and by extension I was denying the truth about who God is. In my attempt to hide my secrets I also hid my true self. As a result, I lost the ability to thrive—to live courageously and fulfill God's purpose for me as a man. I have found this to be true not just for myself but for other men as well.

I have mentored or discipled men for twenty years. I started working with high school boys and young adult men through the ministry of Young Life. Then, as I built relationships with business leaders in the community and worked with the local Young Life Committee, I discovered the same trends among men, regard less of age. It was surprising at first how these men, with families who were senior to me, who seemed so much more successful and mature than me, would confess that they still struggled with fear and insecurity in the same ways I did—insecurity about their marriage, disappointment with their career, or simply feeling incompetent as a man because of father wounds. Regardless of how successful or put-together they looked on the outside, the undercurrent of disempowerment eventually made itself known in our conversations.

After Young Life, I was asked to become the men's pastor at a large church in Pittsburgh where it became my full-time job to think about men's discipleship. Once again, the same consistent and persistent theme of disempowerment played out in nearly every man I encountered.

Currently, as the National Relationship Generator for CLC, a men's discipleship ministry, I consult with pastors and church ministry leaders about men's discipleship. It shouldn't have surprised me, but not even male pastors are immune to this epidemic of disempowerment. Often the first step to effective men's discipleship in a church is for the *pastor* or *ministry leader* to step out of the dark and into the light themselves. Most pastors I know understand the struggle of keeping up appearances in order to maintain the trust of their congregation. God forbid they confess to struggling with sin. I was caught off guard by how pastors would confide in me as a fellow pastor because I was an outside, objective party and wasn't tied to their community. They felt the freedom with me to come up for air for the first time in a long time and admit they were struggling with disempowerment.

So, what does it mean to be disempowered? The Latin root *dis* means a "lack of, not," as in dishonest, or "apart, away" as in discard. The root of *empowered* is "power," which means to have the faculty or ability to do something or act in a particular way.

Dis-empowerment means to lack power or agency, or to be deprived of power, authority, or influence. Someone who is disempowered is weak, ineffectual, or unimportant.

One of the best biblical examples of a disempowered man is Samson in Judges 16. Samson's live-in girlfriend, Delilah, tricked him into telling her what the secret to his superhuman strength was—his long hair. He told her that he would lose his strength if his hair was cut short. Samson didn't know that Delilah was a spy for the Philistines, Israel's archenemy. While Delilah kept Samson sleeping, the Philistines shaved his head and he lost his strength. The Philistine army was then able to subdue him. They gouged out his eyes and enslaved him.

Samson was now blind, and no longer had his super-strength because "the LORD had left him" (Judges 16:20). He was helpless, powerless to do anything about his situation and powerless to serve God the way he had originally been called to do. Samson had been disempowered.

In his fantastic book *The 5 Masculine Instincts*, Pastor Chase Replogle vividly describes Samson's predicament:

> The miraculous gift of God's calling and purpose dis-integrated into this: A blind prisoner, shackled and enslaved. The path of self-pursuit always leads to this place. Our faith becomes manipulative. Our senses are

eventually dulled. Our vocation is sold into slavery . . . where God is abandoned and self becomes center, the whole world begins to contract. It has all been a trap. We are betrayed. We betray ourselves.[1]

Like Samson, most of us, as men, are disempowered because we refuse to come into the light and become prisoners to the dark. We fake it and pretend like we own the place. The truth is: we're hiding. The darkness has become our refuge and we've gotten too complacent with its disempowering lies.

This disempowerment often looks like a deep, sometimes subconscious insecurity that manifests in a fight-or-flight response to anything that threatens to reveal the shame we work so hard to conceal. We feel inadequate and incompetent at home and in our marriages. We live duplicitous lives, lacking a centered identity that would otherwise provide the fortitude we need to lead our families well or maintain personal integrity.

The sins of our forefathers haunt us and steal our confidence. We fail to see the meaning and purpose in our careers. We're drowning in a sea of shallow acquaintances, and isolated from any deep, meaningful connections. However, you would have been hard-pressed to get me to admit any of this because the risk was too great that I would lose everything.

Does any of my story resonate with you? Maybe, like me, you are tired of hiding? Are you worn out from carrying the burden of shame and guilt? Is the dissonance between who you really are and who people think you are tearing you apart?

Keep reading. I believe God is about to do a mighty work in your life.

The feedback I received from a friend who read this introduction before it was published was that it made him feel bad about himself. My guess is that you might be feeling similar, so allow me to take a moment to encourage you before moving on.

I love sports, and I'm a very competitive person, so it can be hard for me to lose. Often when I'm playing Ping-Pong or cornhole and I keep falling behind in the score, I will joke around by saying, "Well, this will only make my comeback win look even better!" Similarly, however bad your current situation is, it will only serve to highlight God's goodness and faithfulness as He works to change you for the better.

Confronting the ugly truth of our sin is only the first step, and God wants to move us quickly forward from there. In fact, Hebrews 4:14–16 says that Jesus empathizes with our weaknesses because he was tempted in every way we've been tempted. As a result, God wants us to approach His throne of grace "with confidence, so that we may receive mercy and find grace to help us in our time of need" (v. 16). God doesn't want us to dwell in the past or fall into despair about our sin. He wants us to walk confidently in his grace and mercy.

First John 2:1 adds, "But if anyone does sin, we have an advocate with the Father—Jesus Christ, the Righteous One. He is the atoning sacrifice for our sins." Jesus empathizes with us in our weaknesses, and he is advocating on our behalf. In a sense, he's like our defense lawyer. In fact, the Bible teaches that Jesus is the judge, jury, defense lawyer, and the one who was punished in our place. This has been a comforting truth for me to dwell on because it leaves no one of consequence to condemn or point the finger at me. God, the only one who ultimately matters, has the last word—and this is where we'll find the empowerment we're looking for.

As one who has walked through this process myself, I can tell you there is so much hope! It's not a coincidence that you picked up this book. God has led you to this very moment. If you feel bad about your current situation, be encouraged that this is evidence of the Holy Spirit at work in your life right now—drawing you out of the dark and back into the light, liberating you from slavery, and empowering you to live a godly life.

How to Use This Book

The purpose of this book is to be as practical and actionable as possible. Therefore, you will find prompts throughout the book that will refer you to resources to help you along the way, wherever you are in your journey to empowered manhood.

You can use this book as an individual, or in a group setting. There are questions and scriptural cross-references at the end of every chapter to help you think through and apply the content to your specific situation. Go to empoweredmanhood.com to see additional free videos where I help you process what God is doing in your life through this book. You'll also find additional follow-on digital courses, as well as recommendations to men's resources and experiences I've seen work in my own life.

Lastly, make sure you join the Empowered Manhood Facebook group, where you can connect with me and other men who are on the same journey. My goal for this group is to help you connect with other men, not just online but also in your local area. You'll find, as you continue to read, that connection with other men is key to empowerment.

I suggest reading a chapter, then using the chapter summary to review what you read. Lastly, use the questions at the end of the chapter as a way to internalize and apply what you've learned. If you're going through this material with a group, these questions will be great prompts for discussion. Then, go to empoweredmanhood.thinkific.com to watch the video associated with that chapter. In these videos, I provide insights and recommend trusted resources to facilitate further study or next steps.

Men, wherever you find yourself as you pick up this book, remember that only God is good and faithful. We are not. In fact, the more desperate your situation, the more hope I have for you because you've been broken, and stripped of any prideful illusions about what you think you have to offer God. Rather, I pray you approach this book like the tax collector in Jesus's parable in Luke 18:9–14. Unlike the arrogant priest who presumed upon God's grace, the shameful tax collector stood at a distance from the temple altar: "He would not even look up to heaven, but beat his breast and said, 'God have mercy on me, a sinner'" (v. 13). Jesus said that it was the tax collector, not the priest, who went home justified before God.

I pray that during your journey you will "grasp how wide and long and high and deep is the love of Christ, and to know this love that surpasses knowledge—that you may be filled to the measure of all the fullness of God" (Ephesians 3:18–19). Amen.

CHAPTER 1

DISEMPOWERED

This, then, is the judgment:
The light has come into the world,
and people loved darkness rather than the light
because their deeds were evil.

—John 3:19 (HCSB)

My Shameful Truth Exposed

I still remember that night sitting on the couch looking out the window of our apartment and wondering if my fiancée would ever come back. I was absolutely overwhelmed by shame. I had really hurt her and there was nothing I could do to help ease the pain I had caused her. She was gone and all I could do was sit there and wait.

Maybe she'd come back? Maybe I could talk to her? Maybe I would lie? Maybe I could hide the truth? I went through all the rationalizations, but there was nowhere to turn or hide from the truth of what I had done. The curtain was pulled back on everything I had hidden for most of my life on this one, tragic evening. The worst part was the awful price my sin would exact on my unsuspecting fiancée. The sound of her painful cries will forever be etched in my memory.

Eventually, after a very long hour, she returned, but that was simply when the misery and pain seemed to escalate for us both. She was so hurt, and yet torn, because at one time I was her strength—her safe place. Now she desperately wanted to find refuge in me again, but I had just betrayed her trust profoundly. It felt like the death of someone she thought she knew. I wanted to wrap my arms around her, comfort her, and provide solace but any movement toward her was rejected—and rightly so. You see, just a few hours earlier she had walked in on me while I was looking at pornography on the computer.

I had desperately struggled with an addiction to pornography since high school and my fiancée had no idea the extent of my secret. I had worked very hard to hide this shameful part of my life. I knew it was wrong, but I was powerless over its control of me. If someone I respected had found out that I did these disgusting and repulsive things in secret, it would have been more than I could bear. Therefore I hid it in the dark, and did everything I could to prevent this secret from coming into the light. No one saw it, but there was always a constant battle between light and dark raging inside of me.

The Battle between Light and Dark

As a child, I vividly remember being scared out of my mind to descend into the dark abyss that was my grandparents' cellar. If the lights were on, I *might* dare to venture down those stairs. However, the lighting wasn't very good, and scary, dark corners abounded where anything could hide and jump out and attack me. Being asked to fetch a can of soup or take a laundry basket down conjured as much fear in me as being confronted by the devil himself.

After making my way down the stairs I would move as quickly as possible past the side of the basement with the crawl space, where I imagined angry, dead people were buried and wanted to pull me in and eat me. Clothes hanging on clotheslines all around cast ghostly shadows on the cement block walls, looking like they were laughing and mocking me. There were old tables and other furniture that needed to be navigated, which gave nasty creatures all sorts of places to hide under before snatching me by the ankle and pulling me down to the underworld. Any unexpected sound at all would paralyze me with fear. Finally, the tingle up my spine seemed to send electrical charges through my whole body, inspiring me to literally sprint back up the stairs to safety. As a result of being in a rush I would often forget something. That meant descending once more, to confront my worst fears all over again!

From a very early age, most of us understand the ominous truth about the darkness. We're scared of the dark before ever being taught that there is anything in the dark to be scared of. It is the unknown, the secrecy, that concerns us. That mystery creates in us a fear of what we can't see or understand. We suspect that what we don't know will hurt us. Most kids feel much more secure with the lights on. Nightlights and leaving the bedroom door cracked provide some relief because it allows light into the darkness and helps reveal what is hidden.

Sadly, later in life, the darkness became my place of hiding, a refuge of isolation where I would indulge my fantasies without fear of anyone finding out. Ironically, contrary to my early childhood experience, I felt safer and more comfortable in the dark than I did in the light. Whether it was making out with a girl on the couch with the lights off or sneaking out at night to vandalize a neighbor's house, I learned to find protection under the cover of darkness.

The older I got, the more sophisticated and insidious the darkness became. I learned how to navigate in the shadows by lying and manipulating others. I would misrepresent other people in order to make myself look better, and I became an expert at gaining people's approval to get what I wanted. Eventually, I became one of the very monsters I once feared as a child, lurking in the dark. The darkness was darkest inside of me.

Somehow, as men, our attitudes about the dark change over time. The light which was once so reassuring becomes threatening, and the dark which was so ominous becomes a place of escape. It's been said that darkness is simply the absence of light. Darkness then, in and of itself, is really nothing but a void. It is nothing, really . . . until we choose to use it to hide from the light. Once we do that, the battle between light and dark begins.

This struggle between light and dark has been going on throughout all human history. In fact, mankind has been telling stories infused with the themes of light and dark, good and evil, since the beginning of time. Award-winning journalist and writer Scott Neuffer says, "Authors have played with the distinctions of light and dark for as long as others have reinforced their separateness."[2]

Themes of light and dark are also used in nearly every religion. An article published by The Center for Critical Research on Religion states, "As a perceptual experience, a metaphor, and an instrument of devotional practice and mystical technique, light in its various modalities—clear, colored, radiant, glowing, shining, and even blinding—has played a central role in histories of Judaism, Christianity, Islam, Manichaeism, and Neoplatonic mysticism, as well as in Buddhist and Hindu esoteric traditions, to name only the most well-studied."[3]

Ancient literature and religions from every culture around the globe have used the metaphors of light and dark to illustrate this

ancient dichotomy. Look at any compelling narrative of any significance and you will find this theme to be ubiquitous, whether
it is implied or explicit. Nowadays, the most compelling themes
of light and dark appear in film. A paper published in 2013 by the
University of Amsterdam highlights three poignant examples: *The
Fellowship of the Ring*, *Apocalypse Now*, and a famous 1926 Ger-
man film, *Faust*.[4]

The Fellowship of the Ring, part of the Lord of the Rings trilogy,
uses bright light to depict the good elves in the city of Rivendell and
contrasts that with the "dark lord" Sauron, who lives in the murky-
looking Mordor. In *Faust*, director F. W. Mernau used bright light
to depict an angel, in contrast to the dark silhouette of Satan. Fran-
cis Coppola brilliantly utilizes light and dark in his film *Apocalypse
Now* when the character Captain Willard (played by Martin Sheen),
is locked up in a dark, underground prison. Another "enlightened"
character, Colonel Kurtz (played by Marlon Brando), sits in broad
daylight as he reads from a report to convince Willard that he (Willard), has always backed the wrong side of the war.

Finally, I don't think any man can think of a more compelling
depiction of light and dark than in the *Star Wars* characters Darth
Vader and Luke Skywalker—especially when Darth Vader pleads
with his son Luke, "If you only knew the pow-wer of the dark side."

From a biblical perspective, it is quite simple: light represents good and darkness represents evil. Light is truth, purity, and
righteousness; while darkness represents lies, evil, and nefarious
activity. This metaphor originated at creation, as Genesis 1:3–4 tells
us: "Then God said, 'Let there be light,' and there was light. *God
saw that the light was good*, and God separated the light from the
darkness."

Interestingly, darkness is not explicitly created by God, but
simply exists as a byproduct of the existence of light. He does

not use any adjectives to describe the darkness; he simply separates the light from the dark. Perhaps that is why God describes light as good and omits any description of the darkness. And yet, as inconsequential as the dark seems to be, it has an incredibly powerful influence over us.

Resigning to the Darkness

While I was still in college, I remember buying the book *Every Man's Battle*, with high hopes of attaining victory over my addiction to pornography. It seemed to offer a fairly simple, straightforward plan—and it even said that if I stuck to the plan, I would see freedom from lust after a few months. However, I was still too dependent on my own willpower and lacked a community of men willing to take the journey with me. Therefore, my attempt at putting the book's strategies into practice failed. After many attempts and failures, I gave in to despair and stopped believing freedom was possible.

Eventually I began to believe that managing my sin and image would be easier. I was already good at that. My thought process was that if I could just keep the number of times I fell to a minimum while managing my image, I could hold out until I was married. Marriage was the promised land. Of course, I now know how foolish this thinking was. I fooled myself into believing the lies I was being sold in the dark. As the Casting Crowns song "Slow Fade" says, "It's a slow fade when you give yourself away." Little by little, piece by piece, the truth was compromised, and I slowly resigned myself to the dark.

To my fiancée, pornography was an issue pedophiles and rapists struggled with. Her Christian fiancé, who was a church staff member and leading a youth ministry, could not possibly be associated with such dark and evil types. So, that day she walked in on me while I was on the computer suddenly caused her to question everything she thought she knew about me, because so much had been hidden from her.

I too suddenly started to question everything I thought I knew about myself because the truth was hidden from even me by the lies of the dark. What I discovered is this: being hidden in the dark, whether it was by myself or with someone else, gave me permission to do things I would never consider doing in the light. This caused me to live my life out of the fear of being found out, which handicapped my faith and stole my confidence.

The darkness I found refuge in was now suddenly stripped away by the light of truth for both me and my fiancée. I could no longer lie to myself or anyone else because the ugly, shameful truth had been revealed. What I didn't realize at the time was that God, in his mercy, had just thrown me a lifeline. It didn't feel like a rescue, however. Rather, it felt more like a violent intrusion. The truth was that God had begun to do something miraculous in my life through the power of his revealing light.

I would eventually learn through this painful experience that only when a man bravely steps into the light of God's truth does he find everything he needs. There is an irony in this: As men, we are taught to be strong, self-reliant, and have no problems or "issues." We're convinced not to expose ourselves to the light. So we cower in the dark, afraid to be found out or have our worst fears realized. We fear others will discover that we don't have what it takes, that we're incompetent—or worse, that we're unworthy of love because of our sin. As a result, we resign ourselves to the dark because there doesn't seem to be another way. We manage our dual worlds as best we can, but it is nearly impossible to completely remove the feeling that things just aren't right.

Inevitably the moment comes when we are confronted with the unmanageability of our sin, just as I was when my fiancée walked in on me. However painful and traumatic, these can be the most honest moments in our lives if we allow them to be. It's only through honestly confronting what we hide in the dark that we find the freeing "pow-wer" of the light.

Disempowered

To be disempowered means to be powerless. In his powerful book *Unmuzzled*, J. S. Shelton compares disempowerment to a muzzled dog: "Just as a muzzle incapacitates a dog. . . . A muzzled man feels restricted and unworthy to pray, seek, and speak to God."[5] The disempowered man is restricted and prevented from taking meaningful action for God's sake. They have been silenced, and they miss out on God's blessing.

Disempowerment thrives in the darkness, where evil things are hiding. What is it that you're hiding? Maybe pornography isn't a part of the dark where you reside. Maybe for you it's alcohol, drugs, entertainment, or gaming. In my experience, 95 percent of the time the root of pornography is pretty close to the root of all of these other vices, which seduce us with fantasy or promise us an escape. They lure us into the dark and capture our imaginations. They short-circuit our ability to endure discomfort and prevent us from cultivating true character.

You probably don't need reminding that the internet, social media, and online gaming have only exacerbated our battle with the dark. Modern media entices us with promises to relieve the pressure of realities we feel incapable of handling. Men would rather live in the fantasy worlds of gaming and virtual relationships than engage with gritty, real-world experiences. One man once told me, "Real life is just too disappointing." No wonder, right?

After spending enough time in the dark, the risk of coming into the light and being exposed is too great—too unbearable for men.

This is especially true when most men in our culture have been taught to hide our weaknesses and insecurities. Yet stepping into the light is exactly how we find the power and freedom to live out our true purpose. In turn, we discover new levels of character and integrity we never thought possible.

Again, I ask you: What are *you* hiding?

If you can't quite answer this yet, you may be wondering what others are hiding. You may not be able to tell from the outside looking in, because men are masters at keeping up appearances. Personally, this made it very hard for me to find authentic connection with other men. We might be faithful attenders at church, involved in our son's or daughter's activities, maybe even killing it at work, but in our quiet moments we feel the deep ache of disempowerment. Thus, you may not even know what it is you're hiding. This is what happens when you are truly in the dark.

Have you chosen to hide in the dark rather than walk in the light? If so, you, like the rest of us, have been disempowered by the lies of the dark which cause us to live out of fear and insecurity. The truth is that becoming the empowered man God intended can only be achieved through what God has already done, not by what *we* do. Maybe you've discovered this the way I did while trying to apply the strategies of *Every Man's Battle* alone.

Men, it is time to stop cowering in the dark and come out of hiding. Our world needs us to bravely step into the light and courageously embrace the truth. Our women and children need men who are humble and well-acquainted with God's grace. Only through walking in the light of the gospel will we become the men our world needs so desperately.

We need courageous men who are convinced of God's goodness—not because we feel self-sufficient or that we have all the answers, but because we are well-acquainted with the God who *is* all-sufficient and *does* have all the answers. Empowered men who have come into the light are humble and gentle because they are keenly aware of their own infirmities. A man like this reflects the character of God who is a refuge for the weak and the vulnerable. We can't be a refuge for others without first finding refuge in God ourselves, in the light.

Our world also needs courageous men of strength who will compete for God's redemptive purposes. However, this strength will not come from us but from the God who redeemed us. We cannot expect to be used by God for his redemptive purposes without first being redeemed ourselves. The first step to empowered manhood is out of the dark and into the light.

Chapter Summary:

- The truth was revealed when my fiancée walked in on me while I was on the computer looking at pornography. Everything I had been hiding in the dark was suddenly laid bare and I was confronted by the destructive nature of my sin.

- The battle between light and dark is well documented throughout history in religions, ancient literature, and media. When we choose to hide in the dark, we forfeit the freedom of the light and give our secrets power over us.

- If we try to fight the battle against the dark in our own strength, we will lose. It is only through confronting the sin and bringing it into the light that we'll experience the freedom and confidence we've been longing for.

- If you've been hiding in the dark, then you're disempowered. The only way to empowered manhood is to step into the light, by entrusting yourself to God.

Questions for Discussion and Further Study

1. Have you ever been exposed unexpectedly, or had something you were hiding uncovered in an embarrassing way? Explain.

2. If you haven't experienced that worst-case, nightmare scenario of being found out, what would it look like if you did? Who in your life would be affected?

3. Where do you see the battle between light and dark in our world? Where do you see it in your own life?

4. Have you resigned yourself to the darkness? What does this look like in your life?

5. Read 2 Samuel 11–12, which tells the story of Israel's king, David, hiding his sin in the dark. After you've read that, read Psalm 51, which is David's response to his sin being exposed.

   • As you reflect on these passages, write your own psalm to God, acknowledging your sin and expressing gratitude for God's forgiveness and mercy. Make sure to include descriptions of God's character that are most encouraging to you.

   • If you're meeting in a group, share your psalms with each other.

Visit empoweredmanhood.thinkific.com for more insights and resources about disempowerment.

NOTES

CHAPTER 2

EMPOWERED MANHOOD

But if we walk in the light, as he is in the light, we have
fellowship with one another, and the blood of Jesus, his
Son, purifies us from all sin. . . . If we confess our sins,
he is faithful and just and will forgive us our sins and
purify us from all unrighteousness.

—1 John 1:7, 9

Acknowledging Our Need

I have an amazing chiropractor whose heart is to "empower" his clients so that they spend less time in his office getting adjusted. The slogan for his business is, "Live Empowered." Having experienced this empowerment through his treatment and training, I can attest to the effectiveness of his strategy.

I used to be powerless at the onset of my back pain. Sometimes I could feel it coming on and other times it would take me by surprise. Then, once my back was "thrown out," I would be immobile for days. It seemed that the adjustments from other chiropractors would give me temporary relief but would never permanently fix the problem.

Then I met my current chiropractor, Dr. Dan, who took a different approach. He still adjusted me, but he also educated me about how my body was designed. I got a crash course in the things that led to my back problems. This took me down an unexpected path. He taught me that my back pain was just a symptom of underlying, more foundational issues with how I moved, whether it was walking, running, climbing stairs, etc.

I learned that poor movement technique, encouraged by modern-day shoes, began with my feet and ankles. My feet and ankles translated that poor technique to my knees, then to my hips, and ultimately to my back. This led to my body compensating in unhealthy ways which only served to compound the problem.

Dr. Dan trained me to stretch and strengthen certain muscular deficiencies in my body that led from my feet all the way to the misalignment of my spine. My perspective grew from being focused just on my lower back to my feet, ankles, knees, and hips. The problem was much more complicated than I had expected. If I wanted a more permanent solution, it would require me to exert more effort into education, training, and submission to Dan's strategy.

As I began to strengthen these muscles through Dan's training and oversight, I began to see him less and less for adjustments. Eventually when I felt my back was a little tweaked and may be vulnerable to being thrown out again, I knew what to do. Whether it was a stretch or an exercise, I knew how to correct it before it got worse. Incidences of back pain became fewer in the long run, because Dan had helped me address the root of the problem.

In a similar way, God calls us to trust him in addressing our root issues as men. Just as I had to admit my lack of knowledge and ignorance in fixing my back problem, we must admit our helpless, spiritually depraved condition. Unfortunately, it is especially hard for us, as men, to admit our need. As a result, we struggle in silence, in secret, in the dark.

Gary Haugen, attorney, as well as founder, CEO, and former president of International Justice Mission, describes the struggle this way:

> Jesus beckons me to follow him to that place of weakness where I risk the vulnerability of a child so that I might know how strong my Father is and how much he loves me. But the truth be told, I would rather be an adult. I'd rather be in a place where I can still pull things together if God doesn't show up, where I risk no ultimate humiliation, where I don't have to take the shallow breaths of desperation. And as a result, my experience of my heavenly Father is simply impoverished.[6]

Many Christian men today are walking around claiming God's faithfulness, but their experience of the heavenly Father is impoverished because of their own pride and self- sufficiency. That is to say: they aren't living empowered but are still disempowered by the lies of the dark.

Empowered through Surrender

I have a friend named Max, who had been struggling through a painful divorce that had brought him to the end of himself. He realized that even though he had attended church for most of his life, he hadn't truly trusted Jesus. His divorce was an agonizing reminder of the unmanageability of his sin.

One day in our church lobby Max came up to me with tears in his eyes as he confessed his sin to me and expressed his struggle. "How do I trust God?" he asked. I grabbed a nearby chair as an illustration and told him that trusting God was like trusting this chair. I can pay homage to the viability of the chair to accomplish its job without ever sitting on it. I could even make all sorts of convincing arguments to myself and others about how strong the chair is, and how everyone should trust this chair without ever putting my own weight on it.

Max, during this time of desperation, was in dire need of the support this "chair"—Jesus—could provide him. Unfortunately, he had never sat in it himself, so he wasn't certain about its stability. Even though he had proclaimed its reliability, he hadn't experienced it. He was walking around the chair, touching the chair, maybe even leaning on the chair. But Max needed to sit on the chair and entrust his full weight to its support in order to experience the maximum benefit. The same goes for our faith. We must put our full weight on God in order to experience his grace.

You see, some men find the chair—faith in Jesus—and sit in it right away. Other men fall on the chair out of desperate exhaustion. Still others continue to wander around the chair, preferring to depend on their own strength, and miss out on all that God has in store for them.

Let me explain this in another way. Jesus, in his famous Sermon on the Mount, said, "Blessed are the poor in spirit, for theirs is the kingdom of heaven" (Matthew 5:3). What Jesus meant by "poor in spirit" was someone who was aware of his spiritually bankrupt condition. Just as I was incapable of helping myself overcome my back pain, we're all incapable of overcoming our broken, sinful nature. In fact, Ephesians 2:1 says we're as helpless as dead men attempting to live again. Utterly powerless.

Jesus is saying that those who are willing to admit this truth are blessed because they will experience God's redemptive power and gain the kingdom of heaven. The kingdom of God is often referred to as the "upside-down kingdom," because the rules that govern it are the reverse of the rules in the kingdom of the world. Therefore, it is through our weakness and poverty of spirit that we gain power and significance in God's kingdom. It is not through what we offer

God—it is only through what God offers us in Jesus. God has provided everything we need (2 Peter 1:3) in Jesus.

God's Power Source for Empowerment

I recall an event from a men's weekend retreat. It was a chilly, drizzly western Pennsylvania night, but the glow from the bonfire was reassuring. For a time, most of the men had to wait in the pavilion shelter for the rain to cease before enjoying the warmth of the fire together. We sang a couple worship songs and heard some encouraging words from one of our speakers to pass the time, while the pitter-patter of raindrops continued on the rooftop. Finally, after a few moments the rain subsided, and we wandered to the fire like moths to a flame.

As men gathered around the fire that evening, experiencing the joy of newfound friendships and camaraderie, a thought occurred to me: that pavilion was a great metaphor for how Jesus has provided for our need. Follow me for just a minute on this one. According to Romans 3:23–24, "all have sinned and fall short of the glory of God, and all are justified freely by his grace through the redemption that came by Christ Jesus." We all, every one of us, are guilty of sinful rebellion against God. I don't care if you're Mother Teresa, Hitler, or somewhere in between.

Isaiah 53:6 says it like this:

We all, like sheep, have gone astray,

each of us has turned to our own way;

and the Lord has laid on him

the iniquity of us all.

Every single human on the face of the earth is guilty of sin before a holy and righteous God, and every single person is deserving of

God's righteous judgment, or punishment. Yet God, out of his love for us, provided a way of escape from that judgment. Romans 6:23 describes the consequences of our sin, as well as the means of our escape, as I'm sure you've heard: "For the wages of sin is death, but the gift of God is eternal life in Christ Jesus our Lord."

That evening at the men's weekend retreat, I was reminded that, like the rain coming down on us was indiscriminate in its affect, so God's judgment is indiscriminate. It doesn't matter who you are—how much money, power, or influence you have—you are subject to God's righteous judgment. And every single one of us is found guilty. However, we must also remember: " God so loved the world that he gave his one and only Son, that whoever believes in him shall not perish but have eternal life" (John 3:16).

Like the men at the retreat huddling in the pavilion, Jesus is the shelter whom God provided for our sin. He is our refuge and safe place. All we're asked to do for redemption is to seek refuge in the shelter of his love and to come out of the rain (see Figure 1).

In effect, God is saying to all of us, "Hey! Everybody in! Come out of the rain! I provided a dry, safe place for you." This is the

foundation for empowerment; it's the rock upon which we build our faith.

Notice that your only role is to run into the shelter. You aren't expected to improve yourself morally in an attempt to earn standing before God—that would be prideful and self-defeating! No matter how hard you try, you're still all wet! Ephesians 2:8–9 says it this way: "For it is by grace you have been saved, through faith—and this is not from yourselves, it is the gift of God—not by works, so that no one can boast." It's not about our own self-improvement plan. All it takes on our part is acknowledging that we're all wet because of our sin and deciding to run to the shelter for refuge.

The Battle between Light and Dark—A New Approach

Israel's first king, Saul, was humble at the beginning of his reign. The prophet Samuel said as much when he told Saul, "Although you were once small in your own eyes, did you not become the head of the tribes of Israel?" (1 Samuel 15:17). We see this humility demonstrated earlier in 1 Samuel 11:5, where it says, "Just then, Saul was returning from the fields behind his oxen." By this point Saul was anointed king over Israel, so why was he still plowing in his field? There could be several answers to this question, but one thing is certain—being anointed king over Israel hadn't gone to his head yet, because Saul clearly didn't think that plowing his field was beneath him as king.

Unfortunately, Saul became prideful as he became bigger in his own eyes and God became smaller. Only recently have I noticed, in 1 Samuel 11, the beginning of what seems to be a self-reliant attitude in Saul.

Israel's enemy, the Ammonites, had besieged the Hebrew town of Jabesh Gilead and everyone was weeping over their plight. This is when Samuel returns from plowing his field to find out the terrible news. First Samuel 11:6 says, "When Saul heard their words, the Spirit of God came powerfully upon him, and he burned with anger." Now, we know that "human anger does not produce the righteousness that God desires" (James 1:20). So, even though the Spirit of God came upon Saul, he wasn't immune to pride or sin. Therefore, what he does next seems to be motivated by ego. Saul basically threatens to kill all of Israel's livestock if they don't follow him and Samuel into battle against the Ammonites (1 Samuel 11:7). God gave Israel victory that day; however, it seems that it was the beginning of the end of Saul's humility.

Later, Saul is so filled with pride and avarice that God tears the kingdom away from him and he goes insane trying to kill David, the next king anointed to take Saul's place. Everything we hear about Saul from 1 Samuel 13 onward is negative. Fear and insecurity ruled over him because he became full of himself and forgot about God's faithfulness. Saul stopped being dependent on God, resigned himself to the dark, and became totally self-reliant.

Most men are convinced that winning the battle between light and dark, truth and lies, is up to them. Much like an athletic competition, a challenge we face at work, or a battle, we feel compelled to muster all of our willpower, energy, and resources to combat it. After all, that is what we've been taught for nearly all our lives.

The reality is, we are completely and utterly powerless in the battle between light and dark. Unlike movies that portray the protagonist as having the solution within themselves, the truth is that the answer is without, not within. We are not going to find our strength to overcome the lies of the dark deep inside of us. In fact, that is one of the lies of the dark that deceives us and keeps us enslaved, just as Saul was enslaved by his pride.

Ephesians 2:1 says that you are "dead in your transgressions and sins." This means there is nothing we can do to make things right. We are *dead*, incapable of justifying ourselves by God's perfect, righteous standards. Colossians 2:13 also describes us as being "dead in your sins." What this means for men today is that, instead of verifying our identity in our achievements, we must live out of our confirmed identity in Christ. Instead of laboring to solve our problems, we must learn to rest in God's solution. Instead of depending on our own wisdom, we must yield ourselves to God's will.

Don't get me wrong; there are most definitely things we must do, of course. However, the main thing we should do is let the gospel (the good news of what Jesus accomplished for us) motivate our actions. Just as I had to submit and entrust myself to the treatment of Dr. Dan, it is our posture toward God and our attitude toward ourselves and others that will avail us of God's work in and through us.

If you are anything like me—you've been losing the battle between light and dark, and don't feel like you have a safe place to run to—you know what this prison of darkness feels like. You are completely at the mercy of your vice. You probably feel powerless to make it right, or are still delusional about how much you can control. The only thing you can do is settle into your new, confined reality, and hope things don't get any worse.

I'm here to tell you that there is a way out. The door to your prison cell has been unlocked and opened by the finished work of Jesus Christ. You are free to go! This is the gospel—the "good news" about how God has saved us, setting us free from the prison of sin and death and empowering us by his Holy Spirit.

So the question is: Have you entrusted yourself to Jesus and taken refuge under his shelter? Or are you still all wet, trying to do things in your own power? The gospel acts like a flashlight or lantern that lights the path ahead, empowering you to move forward in the dark, discover God's purposes, and experience the freedom of the truth.

Three Stages of Empowered Manhood

So let's define what it means to be an empowered man. A man who is empowered is one who has stepped into the light of God's truth, either voluntarily or by force. He's been humbled by a desperate dependence on God for the forgiveness of his sin, and continually relies on the Holy Spirit's work in his life. The empowered man has all his weight firmly planted in the chair of God's grace and is convinced of God's faithfulness because he has experienced it for himself. Finally, the empowered man has given himself to God's purposes rather than to his own agenda.

In my personal experience of redemption and faith, and my experience working with hundreds of other men, I have identified three stages of empowered manhood. An empowered man is a man who is 1) known by God, 2) grown by God, and 3) owned by God. Understanding these three stages have helped me and many others by giving us a framework for understanding our experience during specific seasons of life. It also reminds us that it is an ongoing, never-ending process.

You could think of these stages as a Venn diagram combined with an ongoing, step-by-step process. Each stage is inextricably linked. They each lead to, or point to, another stage. They are interrelated and even interdependent on one another. We can always find ourselves somewhere within each of these spheres, and yet also within all of them at the same time. We can choose to focus on one at a time, or step back and see a bigger picture of how God is working in our lives through all of them at the same time.

The next three chapters of this book will go into detail about the stages of empowered manhood, but let me offer a short explanation of each of them now before moving on.

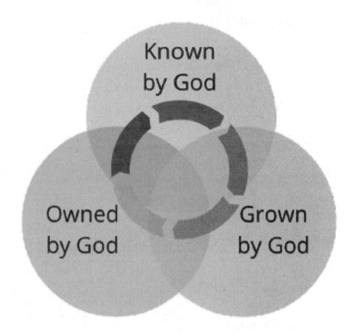

The first stage of empowered manhood is being *Known by God*. This means that a man has surrendered to God and entrusted himself to Jesus for the forgiveness of his sins. This is very different from the man who is still living in his own power and strength. God knows the empowered man very differently than he knows the self-sufficient man.

The second stage of empowered manhood is being *Grown by God*. The man who has placed his faith in Christ's finished work receives the gift of the third person of the Trinity, the Holy Spirit. If running into the shelter is plugging yourself into the power source, the Holy Spirit is the power that runs through the cable and brings a man back to life. The idea of "self-help" is foreign to the empowered man because he understands that God himself, through the Holy Spirit, accepts responsibility for his moral improvement and character development.

Lastly, the empowered man is *Owned by God*. This man is no longer his own but is a tool in the hand of the God of the universe to use at his disposal. Eventually the empowered man is submitted to the will of God, versus his own will, which leads to the greatest purpose and fulfillment a man could experience.

Chapter Summary

- Acknowledging our need, the way I did with my chiropractor, is essential to being empowered. Our pride and self-sufficiency only lead to an impoverished relationship with the Father.

- Only once we put our full weight, or trust, in the chair—that is, place our faith in Jesus—will we *experience* God's faithfulness. It is through our weakness and poverty of spirit that we gain power and significance in God's kingdom.

- The source of our empowerment is dependency on God's provision for our sin. Our self-improvement plan is self-defeating. God has already provided a refuge for us in Christ.

- The battle between light and dark is a battle God has already won. We are empowered through God's provision, not by mustering our own efforts.

- The three stages of empowered manhood are being known by God, grown by God, and owned by God.

Questions for Discussion and Further Study

1. Have you acknowledged your need for God? In other words, do you believe you are "poor in spirit" like Jesus says in Matthew 5:3? Why or why not?

2. In what ways have you been self-reliant? It may be helpful to think about the chair or pavilion illustrations.

   - In what ways have you been circling the chair, yet not entrusting your weight to it?

   - Are you all wet, standing outside the shelter? What does that look like, for you?

3. How would you describe your battle between light and dark? Have you seen victory and experienced freedom, or has it been an ongoing struggle?

4. How does it feel to know that your moral improvement and character development are God's responsibility?

5. Write your own definition of empowered manhood.

Visit empoweredmanhood.thinkific.com for more insights and resources about empowered manhood.

NOTES

CHAPTER 3

STAGE 1: KNOWN BY GOD

The true light, who gives light to everyone,
was coming into the world. . . .
The Word became flesh and took up residence among us.

—John 1:9, 14 (HCSB)

Does God Know You?

My grandfather was a rags-to-riches story in the coal industry of the Ohio Valley, where he made an indelible mark in the lives of thousands of families. In 1943 he went to work for Hanna Coal Company, a division of Consol Coal Company, as a billing clerk. In 1967 my grandpa, Ralph Hatch, took the helm as president of Hanna, the largest division of Consol at the time.

Then, in 1973, he was named vice president of safety at Consol, where he helped them become #1 in safety in the United States. Grandpa became a spokesman for Ohio's surface mining industry and diligently worked with state and federal government officials to improve mine safety.

One of Grandpa's colleagues, Robert Johnson, a safety VP at Continental Oil Company, said, "Many funerals have never been held, many children still have their fathers, all because of Ralph Hatch and his dedication to safety."

I still remember going on shopping trips or running errands with Grandpa around town and it never failed that we would run into someone who knew him and was grateful for his influence on their lives. Grandpa always cared deeply for others and had a unique way of making people feel special. Everyone loved my grandpa and that made me feel really special to be his grandson.

As much as my grandfather loved those miners and their families, his relationship with them didn't compare to his love and devotion to me and his other grandchildren. We were his grandchildren, and that entitled us to privileged treatment. This included staying overnight at my grandparents' house, eating meals with him and Grandma, going on exciting trips with them, and playing with modeling clay for hours on their kitchen table.

Grandpa also took a very active interest in our activities, like sports. He bought a video camera and came to just about every athletic event to record my football games and track meets. I'm so grateful for his efforts to capture amazing memories on video that I still have today.

Unlike the many mining families Grandpa cared so much about, he knew us very differently as his grandchildren. He is our forefather. I was the future of the Hatch family name and the torchbearer of our family legacy. As a result of my grandpa's love, I lived with unquestioned confidence about my identity as his grandson. I enjoyed a privileged position because Grandpa knew me.

In a similar yet more profound way, God knows you differently if you've trusted Him, and this leads to certain privileges and security in our identity as God's beloved sons and daughters. Even in our sin, God directs our circumstances and consequences for his righteous purposes and for our good (Romans 8:28).

I look back at the day my fiancée walked in on me while I was looking at pornography as the day that God humiliated me into a desperate dependence on him. He graciously pushed me into the light that I had been avoiding for so long. In doing so he revealed the truth about my sin, but he also revealed the glorious truth about who I am because of his grace. It was tragically unfortunate and painful that I had to be pushed, but it was the beginning of a whole new life of freedom and joy of being known by God.

The most vital piece to this newfound freedom and joy in the light was understanding my identity in Christ. What I mean by identity in Christ is: who God says I am as a result of entrusting myself to him for the forgiveness of my sins, and redemption of my soul. Now that I am part of God's household, much like I was part of my grandpa's household, I have a new identity because I am known by God.

You may be wondering, didn't God already know you? After all, Mike, he knows everything, right? And he knows everything about everyone.

That is correct. He definitely knows us. In fact, Jeremiah 17:10 says,

> I the LORD search the heart and examine the mind, to reward each person according to their conduct, according to what their deeds deserve.

Oh yes, God knows us all right. But if you haven't trusted Jesus for your salvation, it looks a little different for you.

Let me illustrate: I love the neighborhood kids and I love my twelve-year-old son's friends. But my relationship with those kids is very different from my relationship with my son.

My son is uniquely my responsibility. I gave him his name, Matteo. He is dependent on me for his very basic needs. He is also uniquely dependent on me for my fatherly affection and love. No other father will ever be able to take my place because Matteo is *my* son.

By the same token, if you haven't come under the submission of the loving and gracious authority of Jesus Christ, you don't enjoy the same intimate relationship with God as your Father. You might be a "child of God" in the generic sense, that he created you, but you are not his child. Once you have entrusted yourself to God through faith in Jesus, you are moved into the house of God. You become dependent on his provision, and abide by his rules.

Listen to what Jesus says about this difference:

> "If you hold to my teaching, you are really my disciples. Then you will know the truth, and the truth will set you free."
>
> They answered him, "We are Abraham's descendants and have never been slaves of anyone. How can you say that we shall be set free?"
>
> Jesus replied, "Very truly I tell you, everyone who sins is a slave to sin. Now a slave has no permanent place in the family, but a son belongs to it forever. So if the Son sets you free, you will be free indeed." (John 8:31–36)

Do you see the contrast Jesus creates here? You are either a slave to sin, or you are a son of God by virtue of what Jesus has done on our behalf through the cross and his resurrection. Jesus is God's firstborn and most highly exalted. No one carries more authority, and by that authority he ushers you into adoption as true sons of the Most High. When we find refuge in God, in the light of his truth you get to know and trust God. Even more importantly, God knows you!

Paul emphasized the significance of God knowing us, compared to the insignificance of what we know:

> But knowledge puffs up while love builds up. Those who think they know something do not yet know as they ought to know. But whoever loves God is known by God. (1 Corinthians 8:1b–3)

No knowledge we could possess compares to God's knowledge of us. In fact, the knowledge we possess can cause pride, while God's knowledge of us produces humility.

Amos discusses this same idea with respect to the chosen people of Israel, "I have known only you out of all the clans of the earth" (Amos 3:2). God only knew Israel? Surely, he had knowledge of other nations around the world. What God meant in saying that he had "known only you" was that Israel was his son. The nation had entered into a covenant relationship with God as his child and God was committed to them uniquely, compared to every other nation. In Exodus 4:22, God says explicitly, "Israel is my firstborn son."

Just as I am uniquely committed to, and responsible for, my son Matteo, God had that kind of relationship with Israel. This was a foreshadowing of what was to come in our own relationship with God through Jesus. This is the unique relationship we enjoy with God in the light, and it will be the defining factor for whether we enter eternity with Jesus, "Not everyone who says to me, 'Lord, Lord,' will enter the kingdom of heaven, but only the one who does the will of my Father who is in heaven. Many will say to me on that day, 'Lord, Lord, did we not prophecy in your name and in your name drive out demons and your name perform many miracles?' Then I will tell them plainly, 'I never knew you. Away from me, you evildoers!'" (Matthew 7:21–23).

So, you may "know" a lot about God, but does God know *you*?

A New Identity

I don't remember anything Buc said as he drove me from one end of town to the other. In fact, he may not have said anything at all. I just remember his presence in the car that day being so powerful during this time of grief and deep loss. Buc was one of my Young Life Leaders who mentored me while I was in high school. He invested a ton of time and energy into me and my friends—sharing the gospel, teaching us the Bible, and loving us through tough times.

I was a teenager, about 17, and nothing had been more traumatic for me in my young life than what I was confronted with in that moment. My parents had just separated and were heading toward an inevitable, messy divorce. After we pulled into a gas station to fill up, my emotions overwhelmed my ability to keep any composure and deep, heaving sobs erupted from inside. Buc simply got back into the car, pulled out, and kept driving toward what felt like a cruel destiny.

The day Buc drove me across town was a day I will never forget. It was one of the most painful days of my young life. It was decided that I would live with my dad at my grandparents' house until my mom moved out and got her own place. This was the first night I would be staying at my grandparents' house, which meant I had to leave my mom behind. The pain of my parents' separation began to set in for the first time, and it felt like I was turning my back on my mother. I was confused, and I questioned everything, including myself.

Even though I don't remember Buc saying anything, he had already said more than enough through his intentional influence in my life up to that point. I was certain of his unconditional love for me through all the time we spent together previously and all that he had invested in me. Buc didn't need to say anything. His simple, reassuring presence communicated that I was valued and loved. Despite painful and confusing messages from the circumstances of my parents' divorce, Buc's presence provided an anchor that grounded my identity.

Most men today aren't known, and we don't have relationships like I had with Buc. As a result, we're set adrift by challenges and tumultuous circumstances with no mooring for our identity. There is no greater anchor for a man's identity than being known by God.

If you are known by God, then 2 Corinthians 5:17 says that you are a "new creation . . . The old has gone, the new is here!" Theologically, this idea is known as regeneration. Regeneration means that God, through Jesus's finished work on the cross and resurrection from the grave, makes us new. He transforms our hearts by giving us new motivations, a new identity, and a new desire to obey him.

In Ezekiel 11:19b–20, God describes regeneration this way:

> I will remove from them their heart of stone and give them a heart of flesh. Then they will follow my decrees and be careful to keep my laws. They will be my people, and I will be their God.

We actually see regeneration in nature with various animals. In fact, there is a whole discipline of medicine devoted to studying this phenomenon, called regenerative medicine. All living organisms have some ability to regenerate, even if it is just the natural healing process where new cells are created to replace the old, dead cells.

Other examples of regeneration are more dramatic. For example, the tiny freshwater animal called the hydra can grow two separate bodies after being cut in half. The Mexican salamander has a backbone that can regenerate the form and function of nearly any limb, organ, or other body part.

However, none of these amazing examples in nature are as miraculous as the regeneration we experience when we entrust ourselves to Jesus. Colossians 1:21 says, "Once you were alienated from God and were enemies in your minds because of your evil behavior. But now he has reconciled you by Christ's physical body through death to present you holy in his sight, without blemish and free from accusation."

Stop and read that one more time. Slowly.

Our new identity in Christ is that we are, "holy . . . without blemish [that means perfect] . . . and free from accusation." That is what God sees when he looks at us now, because of what Christ did for us.

Other passages use the idea of adoption (Romans 8:15; Galatians 4:15; Ephesians 1:5) to describe this new reality of who we are as beloved sons, known by God. I envision God holding us in his hands, presenting us like the proud father of a newborn baby, "holy in his sight, without blemish and free from accusation."

In Christ Led Communities (CLC) we call this the "exchanged life." There is a transaction that occurs for anyone who places their faith in Jesus. He takes our sinful brokenness and we receive his righteousness. He bears the punishment for our sin by dying on the cross, and we enjoy God's favor as his perfect and righteous sons. We exchange our sin for Jesus's righteousness.

Sounds too good to be true, doesn't it? But wait, there's more!

God then empowers us through the Holy Spirit, the presence of Jesus living within us, so that we can live according to the truth of this good news. And trust me, we need the Holy Spirit to accomplish this. Past sin may come back to haunt us, or other people in our lives may try to bring up our past sins. Satan will use whatever means possible to accuse and deceive us into thinking that God cannot be trusted—"He is not who he says he is, and you are not who he says you are."

This is where God's Word (the Bible) and church are so important. We need to be steeped in the truth of the Scriptures, which the Holy Spirit within you will use to affirm these truths and strengthen your faith. We need to be immersed in community with other Christians where we learn how to obey and experience the love of God through others. Romans 12:2 describes this process as being "transformed by the renewing of our minds." Our minds are renewed as the Holy Spirit confirms God's faithfulness through these disciplines.

Buc continues to mentor me to this very day, and he still reminds me of the truth of who I am in Christ. His perspective still means a lot to me, but being known by God has more influence on me now by far. The more convinced we are of God's unconditional love for us, and of our new identity in Christ, the more confident we become in other areas of our lives—not confident in ourselves, but in God's faithfulness because of what he has done. This new confidence eventually translates to our vocation, our marriage, our parenting, and every other relationship in our lives.

The Chosen

Recently the highly rated television series *The Chosen* has had quite an impact on both believers and unbelievers alike. Paid for through a record-breaking crowdfunding campaign that raised $13 million dollars, *The Chosen* earned an IMDb rating of 9.7/10 and a 99% audience score from Rotten Tomatoes.

The premise of the series revolves around Jesus choosing his disciples. The film depicts a very relatable Jesus, as well as gritty, down-to-earth disciples with many foibles.

Dallas Jenkins, the producer, does a fantastic job of making all the characters feel real, unlike previously stoic or reserved cinematic depictions of the disciples and Jesus. As you watch the series you may wonder what Jesus was thinking in choosing such misfits to be his followers—but that is the whole point. In fact, that is the point to the whole biblical narrative: to demonstrate how sinful and desperate mankind is in contrast with God's unmatched righteousness.

Unfortunately, we often read the Bible like we read fables. We see the characters in the story as examples of virtuosity and try to imitate them, or apply lessons we learn from them in our lives. This is not the purpose of Scripture. If this is how you approach the Bible, you are likely to get confused—because these people who are supposed to be our role models keep doing shocking and horrifyingly evil things.

Adam and Eve's son Cain kills his brother Abel. Abraham sleeps with his maidservant Hagar, at the behest of his wife Sarah. Later, Abraham allows Sarah to be taken as a sex slave for Pharaoh in order to save his own skin. David, the king of Israel and the one who killed Goliath, stole another man's wife and then had him killed to cover it up. Not to mention that Israel, as a nation, worshipped other gods that demanded child sacrifice and sexual abuse. God often called them out for exploiting the weak and vulnerable in the same way they were previously exploited as slaves in Egypt.

The drama of the Bible is written in such a way to constantly point back to God as the main character and hero. Over and over another person in the narrative is offered as a possible messiah, or savior, and every time they fail spectacularly and are added to the ever-increasing ash heap of sinful humanity.

All of the main characters in the Bible from Abraham to Moses, Daniel to David, Samson to Peter, reveal their repulsive and shocking, sinful nature. One is left feeling somewhat discouraged and disappointed with humanity as a very poor example of moral character. But that's the point. The purpose of the biblical narrative is to cause the reader to wonder if there will ever be a messiah—someone who is finally able to save humanity from our desperate plight.

Of course, that's where Jesus comes in. It took God becoming a human with flesh on to save humanity from our sin. That was the "gotcha" moment of all gotcha moments. God's plan was not to use a human as a sacrifice, but to sacrifice himself, as a human.

He did this because there was no way we were able to save ourselves. There was no way we could meet God's standard of holiness. Now, when God chooses us, he's not choosing us as a result of our own righteousness, moral standing, or amazing character. He's choosing us on the basis of the great exchange, where we are given Christ's righteousness and he accepts our sin.

In the Old Testament, when God told Israel they were going to be his chosen people, he was clear in telling them that it wasn't because of how great they were. Instead, it was because of how great *God* was. This God is the One who knit them together in their mother's womb (Psalm 139:13). He freed Israel from slavery in Egypt by mighty works that displayed his power and sovereignty (Exodus). He provided for Israel's every need until they arrived in the Promised Land, where he defeated all their enemies and set them up to be his ambassadors. God saved Israel from catastrophe, disciplined them like a loving father, and demonstrated his self-sacrificial nature through the symbol of the sacrificial system that foreshadowed his own sacrifice on mankind's behalf.

Deuteronomy 7:7–8 says,

> The LORD did not set his affection on you and choose you because you were more numerous than other peoples, for you were the fewest of all peoples. But it was because the LORD loved you and kept the oath he swore to your ancestors that he brought you out with a mighty hand and redeemed you from the land of slavery, from the power of Pharaoh king of Egypt.

The same is true for us today. God did not choose us on the basis of our own merit, but on the basis of God's love and faithfulness.

This truth should be incredibly freeing and confidence-building—at least as freeing as I felt being my grandpa's grandson, convinced of his unconditional love for me. Yet my grandpa was sinful himself! So if my grandpa was sinful and loved me like that, imagine the security we should get to experience as God's chosen and beloved sons.

This is what Jesus meant when he said, "If you, then, though you are evil, know how to give good gifts to your children, how much more will your Father in heaven give good gifts to those who ask him!" (Matthew 7:11).

This takes the pressure off because, as men, we have nothing left to prove to anyone. We're already proved righteous by God, the only one who matters—through his effort, not ours. We find true rest in being known by God, and this is where a man's confidence should be rooted.

Chapter Summary

- When we trust God for our salvation, we become his beloved sons and privileged children. God knows us differently than the rest of his creation, and we become uniquely dependent on him.

- As true children who've exchanged our sin for Christ's righteousness, we become a new creation. The more convinced we are of our identity in Christ, the more confident we become through the power of the Holy Spirit at work within us.

- Our confidence should be rooted in the fact that God chose us, not that we are righteous enough to earn God's favor. The whole of the Bible exemplifies this truth through the moral failure of every single person—except Jesus.

Questions for Discussion and Further Study

1. What characteristics of God's goodness do you think you've missed as a result of being in the dark instead of walking in the light?

2. If you felt the same security in your relationship with God as I felt in my relationship with my grandpa, how would that change you?

3. Reflect on the scriptures below about your identity in Christ. Discuss, or write down, the attributes of your identity that mean the most to you.
   - 1 Peter 2:9–10
   - Galatians 3:26–29
   - 1 John 3:1–10

4. Write down and/or share the things from your sinful nature that you'd like to exchange for Christ's righteousness.

5. In your own words, describe what it means to be a "new creation" (2 Corinthians 5:17).

Visit empoweredmanhood.thinkific.com for more insights and resources about being known by God.

NOTES

CHAPTER 4

STAGE 2: GROWN BY GOD

For it is God who works in you to will and to act in
order to fulfill his good purpose.

—Philippians 2:13

A Miraculous Work

While I was an area director for Young Life in northwest subur-
ban Chicago, I got to know a high school kid named Chris. He
is one of those miracles of God that I got to watch happen right in
front of me.

Chris grew up with a severe stuttering problem. His parents
told me how they struggled, hauling him from one doctor and spe-
cialist to another, with very few answers. Eventually Chris began to
talk, but it was very few and far between. He was so self-conscious
about his stuttering that he just wouldn't speak at all.

I took Chris to a Young Life camp in Minnesota one summer
with a group of high school kids, and this is no exaggeration—he
did not speak for the vast majority of the week. He may have said a
few words to his friends, but otherwise we couldn't get him to say
anything.

Now, Young Life camp is renowned for being one of the *best* weeks of a kid's life. But if that was true for Chris, we had no idea. We had an absolute blast that week, but you wouldn't have been able to tell by watching him.

He was simply a wall of expressionless silence.

However, on the bus ride home from that camp, Chris decided to step into the light by opening his Bible and reading. In the light of God's truth he found the confidence he had been missing his whole life. He was convicted by the truth of the gospel and decided to devote himself to Jesus's teaching. Chris immersed himself in Scripture, reading every day without fail and exposing himself to the light of God's truth.

Then the miracle happened. Chris began to speak . . . in full sentences! However, it wasn't his own words but the Word of God that he had stored up in his heart. We would have discussions in Bible studies, and Scripture would pour from Chris's mouth. I had never seen anything like it. God gave Chris His words. It was amazing.

Chris not only gained freedom from his stuttering problem, but he was also free to be himself because of the security he had found as a beloved son of God.

Men, as we walk in the light, instead of hiding in the dark we experience God's grace in ever-increasing amounts. This results in greater confidence in the goodness of God, as well as growth in the fruit of the Spirit (Galatians 5:22–23). First John 1:5–7 adds:

> This is the message we have heard from him and declare to you: God is light; in him there is no darkness at all. If we claim to have fellowship with him and yet walk in the darkness, we lie and do not live out the truth. But if we walk in the light, as he is in the light, we have fellowship

with one another, and the blood of Jesus, his Son, purifies us from all sin.

If we are willing to be honest and vulnerable, to step out into the light and acknowledge our sin, throwing ourselves on the mercy of God, He is faithful and just to forgive us and restore us through the blood of Jesus. This process is what led to Chris's life change and newfound confidence that was rooted in Jesus, not in himself.

In the light we are freed by God from our sin, which no longer needs to follow us around like a dark cloud. We can live with confidence, knowing that our standing before God is completely secure because it isn't dependent on anything we've done or do.

But that is only the beginning! Then God begins to work through his Holy Spirit to change us miraculously from the inside out. As a pastor, I have the opportunity to see this happen over and over again.

The Oxygen We Breathe

I ran track in both high school and college. My specialty was the 300-meter hurdles in high school and the 400-meter hurdles in college. There was just something about having barriers in front of me that motivated me. I was never a superstar but was fast enough to earn a co-MVP award my senior year of high school and got to be a part of the Northeast Conference championship team at Robert Morris University.

I continue to enjoy running to this day, but I don't run sprints anymore. Now, I run 5Ks, which demand a different kind of endurance. This made me think about the role that oxygen plays in running, or any athletic pursuit for that matter.

Whether you like it or not, you and I, and everyone else on the planet, is completely dependent on oxygen for our survival. There's no getting around it. However, there are some who embrace this truth and endeavor to become especially dependent on it. These people choose to push themselves to the breaking point, trusting that oxygen will be there for them.

As these people train harder and harder, their bodies miraculously expand their ability to make more efficient use of oxygen. Their lungs change to accommodate greater and greater amounts of oxygen to transmit through their bloodstream and provide for their muscles. This, in turn, translates to better performance athletically than the average person.

Grace works in a similar way. The truth is, we are all desperately dependent on God's grace, or unmerited favor. As I previously mentioned, we are desperately sinful and in need of a savior. This saving grace in Christ is known as "special grace."

Theologians also refer to something known as "common grace," which describes the grace every human experiences but which doesn't necessarily lead to salvation. This includes things like experiencing the benefits of creation, the beauty of a sunset, the joy of relationships, the blessings of childbearing, our heart pumping blood to the rest of our body, etc. This is grace that is common to everyone and we're all dependent on it, like oxygen. The apostle Paul speaks about this common grace in Romans 1:20: "For since the creation of the world God's invisible qualities—his eternal power and divine nature—have been clearly seen, being understood from what has been made, so that people are without excuse."

Saving grace, or "special grace," is the grace a man experiences who has decided to walk in the light, acknowledge his sin, and repent. Similar to the athlete who has a very different relationship to oxygen than the overweight guy stuck on the couch, the empowered man has stepped out into the light and trusted God's grace with much greater levels of dependency. Oxygen is available to both men, just as grace is offered to everyone, but the one who is more dependent experiences exponentially more benefit.

In addition, just as the trained athlete's body responds to intense training, so the godly man responds to God's saving grace through the miraculous work of the Holy Spirit, changing him from within. This is the mystery, and the incredible blessing, of how the Holy Spirit works on our behalf to appropriate larger amounts of grace.

My high school friend, Chris—the one with the stuttering problem from the opening story—decided to take God at his word and trust that the oxygen, or grace, would be there when he needed it. As he took steps of greater dependency on God's grace, the Holy Spirit expanded his capacity for that grace, and Chris grew stronger in faith. His stronger faith in God led to less concern about other's opinions of him and this gave him the confidence to speak.

The Paradox of Faith for Men

The challenge we men face with this idea of dependence on grace comes as a result of believing we can earn it. This is where the analogy of oxygen breaks down. One could assume that because of their great effort, discipline, or willpower, they have earned their faith, and approval from God. This is a fatal mistake many men make.

We are not entitled to grace in the way that we may feel entitled to oxygen. Remember, we are hostile toward God, and our sinful desire is to be our own God. Our default setting is that we hate God and want to kill him, and then assume his throne ourselves. Therefore, God has every right to simply wipe us out of existence. As the only pure, good, and righteous God, he is worthy to judge us guilty and punish us by depriving us from the oxygen of grace.

Yet he doesn't. Otherwise, it wouldn't be grace.

God is good and merciful and loving. His desire is to redeem us from our sin and reconcile us to himself by accepting the punishment for our sin. The grace we enjoy is most certainly unmerited favor. We absolutely do not deserve it and are not entitled to it. Listen to what the prophet Isaiah says:

> But he was pierced because of our rebellion;
> crushed because of our iniquities [sin];
> punishment for our peace was on him,
> and we are healed by his wounds.
> We all went astray like sheep;
> we all have turned to our own way;
> and the LORD has punished him
> for the iniquity of us all. (Isaiah 53:5–6, CSB)

Read that passage again if you need to. Let it sink in. I would recommend you go to your Bible and read the entirety of Isaiah 53 which describes, in perfect detail, the exchanged life we enjoy as a result of Jesus's sacrifice.

So, you see, we should be humbled and feel tremendous gratitude for the gift of grace and how it can empower us as men to live a godly life. We should do our best to do as Paul says in Philippians 3:16: "Only let us live up to what we have already attained"— because we didn't attain this on our own; it was a gift of God (Ephesians 2:8).

This is the paradox.

By God's grace we have already received his favor and unconditional love. Now, Paul says, let's live like that's actually true, never taking it for granted. Let's strive to experience the full benefit of God's grace, as would a runner with oxygen. Let's become ever more dependent on that oxygen to strengthen our faith and improve our performance.

However, let's never forget that our ability to do so is a gift of grace to begin with. And it's only through the miraculous work of the Holy Spirit that we experience the benefits of our effort. From beginning to end, "it is God who works in you to will and to act in order to fulfill his good purpose" (Philippians 2:13).

One of the ways to apply this paradox, as men, is with regard to our physical strength. Men, by and large, are created stronger physically. Yet, God did not grant us that strength (via common grace) for our own glory. We were not created with certain physical advantages so that we could submit other weaker people to ourselves. Rather, God granted us our strength to protect the weak and the vulnerable, to endure suffering in its various forms, and to provide for others.

With this in mind, the cross of Christ is the most breathtaking expression of power and strength the world has ever seen. God with flesh on, Creator of the universe and eternally powerful, submitted himself to torture and execution for the benefit of us who are infinitely weaker and miserably sinful. That is the true, godly expression of strength.

In the same way, we should seek to build our physical and spiritual strength for God's self-sacrificial purposes of redemption. However, if our pride has convinced us that we have earned God's favor, we will sabotage these purposes and cause great suffering for others. Jesus suffered on our behalf to be a blessing to us. We too, as men, are called to suffer on behalf of, and for the benefit of, others.

Whether we suffer the thorns and thistles of life in producing value through hard work, taking a bullet for a friend, or suffering persecution for our faith, this is how we are to lead as men—not as conquerors ourselves, but as conquered by God's grace and submitted to his purposes. Not as a demonstration of our strength, but as a demonstration of God's strength through our weaknesses.

A man who is grown by God is a man who has been humbled by God's gracious provision for sin and committed to a desperate dependence on God's grace. He is painfully aware that the growth of his faith is the result of the work of the Holy Spirit within him, not based on his own effort. This strength a man develops from a greater dependency on God's grace is for God's self-sacrificial purposes. It is for God's glory, not his own.

Helpless

Probably one of the most vivid descriptions of the Spirit's work is in the Old Testament book of Ezekiel. Throughout the book you read about how the Spirit would lift Ezekiel up and bring him to this place or that. Then the Spirit would fill him, and he would speak the words of God to the rebellious people of Israel. It is literally as if Ezekiel didn't have a will of his own but instead was carried along by the Spirit of God.

There is one particularly exceptional example in Ezekiel that highlights just how powerless we humans are, and how dependent we are on God. Ezekiel 37 is the account of "Ezekiel and the Valley of the Dry Bones." Once again God's Spirit brought him and set him down, this time in the middle of a valley where he was surrounded by dry bones.

The point of mentioning the "dry" bones was to emphasize how long they had been there. These people had been dead for a long time—so long, in fact, that the bones had been dried out by years of the sun beating down on them.

God asks Ezekiel, "Son of man, can these bones live?" Ezekiel responds, "Lord GOD, only you know" (v. 3, HCSB).

You can almost sense the exasperation in Ezekiel's voice. What is God actually asking him? Does he want him to do something about the dry bones? Why would he ask him if the bones could ever live again? I'm sure Ezekiel is feeling very sad about the scene. It probably seemed completely hopeless. So Ezekiel, in a sense, throws his hands in the air and says, "I don't know, God. How *should* I know? Only you know."

Then God says to Ezekiel, "Prophecy concerning these bones and say to them: Dry bones, hear the word of the LORD!" (v. 4). Then God tells him to tell the bones that God will put them back together—that he will make tendons and muscles appear, and that skin will enfold them once again. So Ezekiel obeys God and begins to prophecy or preach to the bones.

Clearly Ezekiel is not in control of the outcome. He has simply been told to do as God commanded and allow God to control the results.

Ezekiel 37:7–8 describes the sound of the bones rattling and moving around. They begin to assemble. Then tendons and flesh appear on the bones, but it says there was no breath in them. They were still dead. So God told Ezekiel to "prophesy to the breath" (v. 9) so that these people would live. Then breath came to them, and eventually the dry bones became a vast, living, breathing army.

God compares the helpless plight of Israel in exile to the dry bones. They were cut off because of their sin and hope for their future had vanished. But God himself had resurrected them and gave them new life. God fulfilled his promise years later when he brought Israel up out of exile and back into their land.

There is no difference between us, as men, and those dry bones. Left to our own, we are cut off from God and have no hope of a future. But by God's power, the power of the Spirit, he breathes new life into us. Therefore, why would we think it's up to us once we're saved? How is it that after being resurrected spiritually from the dead, we would think we have anything of value to offer God?

At this point many men will be offended because they don't want to hear that they have nothing to offer God. They want some satisfaction or reassurance that they have done something to warrant his approval and favor, but this only serves to stroke our ego. Our desire to earn our standing before God is simply pride and another example of our rebellion against his good purposes.

The truth is, it is God who grows us. This should provide incredible hope and comfort because he's responsible for our growth plan, not us.

You Don't Have God—God Has You

Recently I had lunch with a friend, John, who owns a relatively successful business. John told me the story of how he started the business and devoted it to the Lord early on in its inception. Even the name of his business unmistakably reflected God's purposes.

Unfortunately, John made some serious mistakes along the way that did not reflect a dependence on God but a prideful self-reliance instead. As a result, the business suffered. Yet, John was humbled by God, repented of his sin, and learned from his mistakes. The Holy Spirit was at work in him to change his heart so that he would more closely reflect God's purposes in the marketplace.

Most men might look at John and be inclined to congratulate him about the success he enjoyed through learning from his failures. Some men might see John as an example to follow in order to avoid some of the same mistakes. We may be tempted to imitate John's habits in hopes to be as profitable in business as he has been. All of this would be a mistake, and would badly distract from the truth.

The truth is that back when John devoted his business to the Lord, it was the Holy Spirit who motivated him to do so. God had already grabbed hold of John and devoted himself to him. The fact that John had devoted his business to the Lord was evidence of God's work in him already.

It is more accurate to say that God had a hold of John much more profoundly than John had devoted his business to God. It turned out that John hadn't truly devoted his business to the Lord, otherwise he wouldn't have been so selfish and self-reliant. He wouldn't have made prideful mistakes that hurt the company.

The good news is, God was more faithfully devoted to John and his business than John was to God. So when John let go because of his own pride and sin, God didn't let go of John. It was God's devotion to John and his business that ensured success, not the other way around.

Allow me to share a couple more compelling examples of this principle of God's faithfulness, this time from Scripture. The first is in 2 Chronicles 6 where Solomon dedicates the newly built temple. The second is Luke 22, where Jesus predicts Peter's denial of him.

In 2 Chronicles 6:22–39, Solomon prays to God, and then runs through a litany of ways Israel will abandon God and suffer the consequences. He specifically mentions famine, military defeats, and even exile. We know all these things eventually occurred, but why would Solomon mention them before they happened? Didn't Solomon, the wisest man who ever lived, know that speaking negativity like that could become a self-fulfilling prophecy?

His point in mentioning Israel's future sin was to highlight God's faithfulness and contrast it with Israel's unfaithfulness. Eventually, when Israel found themselves in exile, or suffering through a famine, they could go back to Solomon's words and remember that they needed to repent and that God would be faithful to restore their nation.

Jesus did something very similar with the apostle Peter in Luke 22:31–34. Jesus tells Peter that he will deny him but that Jesus has prayed for him, that his faith won't fail. Then Jesus tells him that when he turns back (repents), he should strengthen the other apostles. Jesus told Peter this so that when it happened, he would be encouraged by God's faithfulness, not his own ability to maintain his devotion. How amazing is that? Jesus knew Peter would betray him, yet he encouraged him *before* he did it! God knows you will sin and offend him as well, and he doesn't respond like we humans do, with resentment or bitterness or anger. Jesus's heart is for you from start to finish.

The apostle Paul discusses what it looks like to be grown by God as we live by the Spirit, in Galatians 5. Paul describes the fruit of the Spirit in verses 22–23:

> But the fruit of the Spirit is love, joy, peace, forbearance, kindness, goodness,
> faithfulness, gentleness, and self-control. Against such things there is no law.

Fruit comes about as a result of a tree being planted in good soil. A combination of nourishing soil, rain, and sunlight produce the fruit as a byproduct. In the same way, the fruit of the Spirit is a byproduct of being planted in the soil of God's Word, nourished through worship, and being exposed to the light of transparent church community, especially trusting relationships with other men. Psalm 1 confirms this when it says that the one who is blessed "delights in the law of the LORD, and who meditates on his law day and night. *That person is like a tree planted by streams of water,* which yields its fruit in season and whose leaf does not wither—whatever they do prospers" (vv. 2–3, emphasis added). Our responsibility as men is to simply sink our roots into God, depend on his provision, and allow him to grow us.

It should give us great hope to know that God is faithful even when we're not. In fact, it is by virtue of the grace we receive in times of disobedience, struggle, persecution, or suffering that God grows us. Therefore, we have no reason for fear or shame. We need only confess our sins and know that God is faithful and just and will purify us from all unrighteousness (1 John 1:9). This is why Paul said, in Hebrews 4:16, "Therefore, let us approach the throne of grace with boldness, so that we may receive mercy and find grace to help us in our time of need."

The empowered man is Grown by God when he recognizes his need for grace, like oxygen, and steps into the light of God's truth. In doing so, he commits himself not to greater willpower or higher ideals, but to a desperate dependence on grace. Eventually, a man does not just abide in God's light, but God's light resides in a man (Ephesians 5:8). This is when a man is Owned by God.

Chapter Summary

- Miracles happen when we expose ourselves to the light of the gospel. The Holy Spirit works to change us through God's Word which leads to confidence, knowing that our standing before God isn't dependent on anything we've done or will do.

- Grace is like oxygen. We're all desperately dependent on it, but the man who exercises greater dependency on God's grace expands his capacity for that grace and grows stronger in his faith.

- The empowered man becomes ever more dependent on God's grace to strengthen his faith and improve his performance. However, this man is humbled by God's gracious provision for sin and uses his strength of faith self-sacrificially.

- We are completely helpless to change ourselves for the better. In fact, we're "dead" in our sin. However, there is incredible hope and comfort in knowing that God has provided a way to bring us back to life, and that he has accepted responsibility for growing us.

- God's faithfulness to us is what sustains us, not our commitment or devotion to him. This produces a confidence in God's character, not in ourselves.

Questions for Discussion and Further Study

1. Like God's work in helping Chris overcome his stuttering problem, what miraculous work do you hope to see God do in your own life?

2. How would you know if you're feeling entitled to God's grace? What attitudes or actions might tip you off?

3. Read Isaiah 53. Create two columns on a sheet of paper, or in a notebook. At the top of the left-hand column write "Jesus," and at the top of the right-hand column write your name. Now, record in each of the columns the things you and Jesus received from the "great exchange." What is most surprising to you about this exchange? How do you think you should respond?

4. Throughout the majority of history, male strength has been used to exploit and abuse the vulnerable. In what ways can you embody the opposite? Be specific.

5. What difference does it make knowing that the Holy Spirit is at work in you and is evidence of God's faithfulness to you?

Visit empoweredmanhood.thinkific.com for more insights and resources about being grown by God.

NOTES

CHAPTER 5

STAGE 3: OWNED BY GOD

But whoever lives by the truth comes into the light,
so that it may be seen plainly that what they have done
has been done in the sight of God.

—John 3:21

Revealed

Imagine, for a moment, that someone was able to see and record your thoughts on a daily basis—everything you think but never say, all your unspoken words, good, bad, or indifferent. All those lustful thoughts about your coworker, every criticism you held back from saying to your wife, all the prideful inclinations from thinking of yourself as more successful than some of your friends. Whether it is about you or other people, this person has recorded all the thoughts from your mind and the meditations of your heart.

Now, let's say that person decided to invite all your closest friends and family over to watch it together, like a movie, complete with popcorn. Your neighbor, your family, your wife, your children—everyone gets to watch your unspoken words and internal dialogue.

After you get past the anger toward the person who did this to you, how would you feel about all those people having access to that private information?

Before you brush this off too quickly, make sure you take time to think it through. Imagine the looks from your kids. Think about the pain on your wife's face. Embrace this mental exercise; really put yourself there in the moment and imagine what it would be like.

Personally, this was my worst fear, that I would be exposed for the fraud I was. It might be cliché, but I relate to the idea that if anyone found out about the real me, I would be finished. I thought that if that happened no one would ever want to be around me again. So I learned, as most men do, how to hide what I was most ashamed of deep in my subconscious mind where it wouldn't threaten me.

Now, read Jesus's words from Luke 12,

> There is nothing concealed that will not be disclosed, or hidden that will not be made known. What you have said in the dark will be heard in the daylight, and what you have whispered in the ear in the inner rooms will be proclaimed from the roofs. (Luke 12:2–3)

I hope that this scripture gives you pause. The truth is, God already knows everything about your inner dialogue, prideful disposition, and silent thoughts. According to Jesus, this will all be revealed on the day we stand before him face to face. All the things we thought were hidden, or kept in the dark, will be revealed by his light.

Obviously, it is not likely that someone other than God will have access to your deepest thoughts and inner desires anytime soon. But what if I told you that God has exposed his own thoughts, demonstrating that same level of vulnerability, with us?

In other words, God has given us access to his deepest and most intimate longings.

How? Through his Holy Spirit.

In 1 Corinthians 2:10–12, the apostle Paul says, "The Spirit searches all things, even the deep things of God. For who knows a person's thoughts except their own spirit within them? In the same way no one knows the thoughts of God except the Spirit of God. What we have received is not the spirit of the world, but the Spirit who is from God, so that we may understand what God has freely given us."

In verse 11, Paul compares the spirit of a man to the Spirit of God. Just as the spirit of a man knows the deepest parts of man, so the Spirit of God knows the deepest parts of God. As men, we only reveal what we want people to see and hold back everything we don't. However, we can't hide from our spirit which knows everything about us, even the things we hide from ourselves in the deepest recesses of our subconscious mind –not even that is hidden from our spirit within us.

Unlike men, God has not held back or hidden himself. He has opened himself up in the most vulnerable ways anyone could, pouring his Spirit into us and giving us access to the deepest parts of himself.

Right now you may be saying, "Yeah Mike, I understand that, but God has nothing to be ashamed of. He's not sinful like we are, and He isn't trying to hide. It's easier for him to be vulnerable." In a sense, you are correct. God has nothing to hide because he isn't sinful. However, this does not diminish the significance of his expression of vulnerability through the Holy Spirit. Remember what Jesus submitted himself to at, and on his way to, the cross—being stripped naked, spat on, mocked, and brutally murdered. This was the price he paid for his vulnerability—to make the Spirit abundantly available to us.

We were embarrassed to step into the light, so Jesus allowed himself to be exposed and humiliated on our behalf so that we would have a safe place in him. Fear of punishment ruled over us, so Jesus endured that punishment we deserved to set us free. We were ashamed of our sin so Jesus became sin on the cross so that we wouldn't be defined by it anymore. God paid a higher cost for the presence of his Spirit than we'll ever know.

Before Jesus's death and resurrection his Spirit wasn't as accessible as it is today. Why? Because God is too pure and holy. For exactly that reason God had to hide the full expression of his presence from mankind because no one can see God and live (Exodus 33:20). His purity would instantaneously incinerate us, because we are sinful and nothing holy may coexist with anything unholy.

Therefore, there was an infinitely impermeable veil between us and God, separating us from his presence. This is why Israel needed priests to represent them, a temple to serve as an access point to God's presence, sacrifices, and ritual cleansing to prepare them to come before the Lord.

When Christ died on the cross, that veil was torn and the possibility was opened to experience God's presence like we never have before. So I ask you: When you consider the lengths to which God went to provide you with the presence of his Spirit, do you still think it was insignificant for him?

The temple is no longer needed as an access point to God's presence, because *we* are now the temple of the Holy Spirit! First Corinthians 3:16 says, "Don't you know that you yourselves are God's temple and that God's Spirit dwells in your midst?" Through the Holy Spirit, we have unprecedented access to God. During no time in all of human history has God been more vulnerable, available, and intensely present. As we'll see, the presence—or absence—of the Holy Spirit in a man's life is a sign of whether a man is Owned by God or not.

The Seal

As I was driving to the grocery store recently, I saw something strange. At first it was difficult to see what was different about the car in front of me. Something was off about the way it looked but I couldn't put my finger on it.

Then it dawned on me: the car was missing any insignia that would identify the automaker. It was very strange at first, but then I started to see more and more cars that had been relieved of the automaker's logo. It seems like this has become a fad, and in some cases, people will replace those logos with a different symbol. I saw one car that had a Transformers logo in place of the Chevy symbol.

That got me thinking about the logos automakers put on their vehicles. Obviously, those logos give notice to anyone who sees them that this is their car. They made this beautiful piece of mechanical engineering, and their logo is meant to bring glory to them as the manufacturer. It also tells others where they can get the same vehicle if they would like.

There really isn't anything manufactured today that doesn't have a logo or insignia of some kind that identifies, and glorifies, the company who made it (or, as in for example the case of China, the country that manufactured it).

In a similar way, God's Spirit is the logo for anyone who is a Christian. The purpose is to bring glory to God and to identify that "new creation" (2 Corinthians 5:17) as belonging to God. Ephesians 1:13–14 says that the Holy Spirit is a seal that signifies God's ownership:

> And you also were included in Christ when you heard
> the message of truth, the gospel of your salvation. When

you believed, you were marked in him with a seal, the promised Holy Spirit, who is a deposit guaranteeing our inheritance until the redemption of those who are God's possession—to the praise of his glory.

As men empowered by Christ, the Holy Spirit, God's most profound expression of His presence, is a seal of ownership, signifying that we are not our own but that we are "God's possession." The apostle Paul confirms this when writing to the Corinthians: "Do you not know that your bodies are temples of the Holy Spirit, who is in you, whom you have received from God? You are not your own; you were bought at a price. Therefore honor God with your bodies" (1 Corinthians 6:19–20). Unfortunately, many people in our culture today, including pastors, take this passage to mean that we need to develop healthy habits for our bodies. Therefore we shouldn't smoke, we should eat healthy, and maintain an active lifestyle. This was not Paul's intent behind this verse.

Yes, there is truth that we need to care for our physical bodies, but that emphasis attached to this verse profoundly reduces the significance of what Paul is trying to communicate about the Holy Spirit. He is trying to remind the Corinthians of the awe-inspiring truth that the actual presence of God now resides inside of us.

This was a monumental shift in understanding the presence of God which, prior to Pentecost, no one could lay claim to. One had to travel from wherever they were in the world to Jerusalem. This was the only place the God of Israel resided, with his people. He was always Immanuel, "God with us," but the fullest expression of his presence was confined to the temple in Jerusalem. Now, the fullest expression of God's presence is found inside his true children (Romans 8:14)—those who are Owned by God.

God's Will Be Done

One of my favorite stories in the Bible is the story of Jesus's interaction with the woman at the well in John 4. Jesus decided to take his disciples north through Samaria on their way to Galilee, something Jews never did. But Jesus knew he was destined to meet this now famous "woman at the well."

Once Jesus and his disciples arrived at the well, his disciples left him alone to go into the town and get food. At this point the woman came to draw water, and Jesus asked her for a drink. This launched them into a conversation through which we discover that this woman had a sketchy reputation. In fact, Jesus and this woman are at the well, in the middle of the desert at the hottest time of the day, because she was trying to avoid running into other people who might scoff at her.

She had the reputation of being promiscuous, moving from one man to another. In fact, she had been married to five different men. However, we only find this out after she offers to expose a tiny sliver of truth to the light, and Jesus uses that to transform her. Through this interaction with Jesus, she discovers that she was Known by God—and then was Grown by God.

After she finds out that Jesus is the Messiah, without thinking twice she runs back into the town to the people she was trying so hard to avoid, the ones who had shamed her and treated her like garbage, to tell them about him. The Bible says that many people from that town came to believe in Jesus. So this woman with a questionable past and a shady reputation is who Jesus used as his vehicle to bring the gospel to Samaria!

You see, she was no longer her own. She believed Jesus when she "heard the message of truth" (Ephesians 1:13), and the Holy Spirit moved her to do something she never would have done previously.

That's because she was now Owned by God and no longer in bondage to her sin. Similar to Ezekiel, the woman at the well was taken by the Spirit to accomplish God's redemptive purposes.

In his best-selling book *Maximized Manhood*, Edwin Louis Cole describes the process this way, "He (God) is the author of our desires. He doesn't just grant us the desires we have, but He authors His desires in us so that He can fulfill them. In that way, He can bring His kingdom to earth through us."[7] God owns us by virtue of his presence in us, but also by accomplishing his will through us on earth as it is in heaven.

The story of the woman at the well is compelling to me because . . . *I am that woman!* Even as a pastor, I am nothing but a dreadful sinner who's left a wake of destruction because of my sinful rebellion. I am only qualified to share this good news as far as I have experienced it myself. In fact, just like the woman at the well, my own experience of God's grace is what motivates me to share the gospel with others. God has authored his desires in place of my own agenda.

Don't get me wrong; I strongly believe in the value of a seminary degree and studying the Bible. However, ultimately, I am not qualified by my seminary degree but by the power of the Holy Spirit inside of me. His Holy Spirit's presence and work in my life is evidence of the fact that I am empowered by God. The only thing that warrants God using me, or anyone for that matter, is that the light of God resides in me. That is what empowers me to transcend myself and make an eternal impact for God's kingdom.

Galatians 2:20 says, "I have been crucified with Christ and I no longer live, but Christ lives in me. The life I now live in the body, I live by faith in the Son of God, who loved me and gave himself for me." I am not my own anymore. I am Owned by God.

Jesus said, "I am the light of the world. Whoever follows me will never walk in darkness, but will have the light of life" (John 8:12).

The Holy Spirit is "the light of life" now residing inside of us. As we spend time in God's Word, and with God's people (the church), the Spirit teaches us and confirms the truth. This is how we are no longer conformed to the pattern of this world but are transformed by the renewing of our minds (Romans 12:2).

The logo of the Holy Spirit is a seal on our heart that bears witness that we are God's new creation (2 Corinthians 5:17). He is constantly changing us from the inside out, causing us to transcend our own selfish insecurities, fears, and desires, and empowering us to accomplish His redemptive purposes.

This is how and why the apostles accomplished all that they did in spreading the gospel all over the globe, by the power of the Holy Spirit working within them. Again, much like Ezekiel, they were moved along by the Spirit to spread the gospel, encourage the churches, train up pastors, endure hardships, and ultimately give their very lives for the sake of the truth residing inside of them.

Remember, just as the woman at the well discovered, it doesn't take much exposure to the light to allow God to work in you. But you need to start somewhere. When the woman at the well acknowledged the truth that she "had no husband" (John 4:17), it was literally the tiniest amount of truth she was willing to reveal. Some commentators even think she said this with deceptive intentions, so her motives might not have even been pure. Yet, Jesus still took that sliver of truth she offered up to the light and used it for her benefit—and for the benefit of an entire town!

A Hidden Life

Franz Jägerstätter was an Austrian conscientious objector during World War II who was executed for his refusal to fight for Nazi Germany. The movie *A Hidden Life* was released in 2019, retelling the grueling story. The film is stunning. I still remember seeing the film and being left speechless for hours afterward. Its title was inspired by a George Eliot quote: "for the growing good of the world is partly dependent on unhistoric acts; and that things are not so ill with you and me as they might have been, is half owing to the number who lived faithfully *a hidden life*, and rest in unvisited tombs."

Throughout the movie, Jägerstätter was given multiple opportunities to change his stance, save his life, and return to his wife and three young daughters. One of the Nazi officers pleads with him, "Just sign this and you will go free." Jägerstätter responds, "But I am already free." Just minutes before his execution he was asked one last time to sign a document to save his life. However, he would not compromise, renouncing any complicity with the Nazi regime. His last recorded words were, "I am completely bound in inner union with the Lord."

The common theme throughout the movie, stated over and over by the Nazis, was that his sacrifice would make no difference. The Nazis reminded him of his impotence to have any effect as they beat him in his jail cell. A couple times during the movie they show a rushing river running through Jägerstätter's little farm town, as if to symbolize evil's swift and overwhelming inevitability. Who was he to try and stand against such a current? He was only one frail man and was sure to be enveloped by the Third Reich and quickly forgotten.

Franz Jägerstätter grew up Catholic, but in the mid-1930s something extraordinary suddenly gripped him and his neighbors were quoted as saying that it was "so sudden that people couldn't understand it." They said it was "almost as if he had been possessed by a higher power." Jägerstätter became very religious and married a woman who was also religiously devout. He was not his own anymore and had clearly yielded his will to God's.

He even traveled to Linz, the capital of Upper Austria, to inquire of his bishop about the Nazi atrocities. Sadly, the episcopate was afraid to confront the issues.

At one point in the film, Jägerstätter visited his local church and met with a painter who was painting icons on the walls and ceilings of the sanctuary. The painter says something profound: "I paint the tombs of the prophets. I help people look up from those pews and dream. They look up and they imagine if they lived back in Christ's time, they wouldn't have done what the others did. . . . What we do, is just create sympathy. We create admirers; we don't create followers. Christ's life is a demand. . . . I paint their comfortable Christ with a halo over his head. How can I show what I haven't lived? Someday I might have the courage to venture. Not yet. Someday I'll paint the true Christ."

The painter was saying that, unlike himself, Jägerstätter was truly owned by God and completely obedient to the demands of Christ, namely his call to sacrifice his life. Jägerstätter embodied empowered manhood because he was not his own and he entrusted himself wholly to God's transcendent purposes. To most observers in his town, this was folly and a waste. In God's economy, however, it is the shunned, the weak, the seemingly insignificant, and the despised who are lifted in honor for all eternity. Those who are admired in this life will be forgotten, swallowed by the ocean of God's redemptive purposes.

Chapter Summary

- Everything we've ever hidden will be revealed by the light of God's truth. However, God led by example in providing access to himself through the Holy Spirit—the most vulnerable expression of his presence in human history.

- The Holy Spirit, the fullest expression of God's presence, is his seal of ownership—a lot like a logo. Just as an automobile logo serves to bring glory to its manufacturer, the Holy Spirit serves to bring glory to God.

- God accomplishes his kingdom purposes through us by virtue of the Holy Spirit inside of us. The Spirit empowers us to transcend our own agenda and accomplish God's will.

- Franz Jägerstätter, an Austrian conscientious objector during World War II, submitted his will to God's to the point of death. He was owned by God and completely obedient to the demands of Christ.

Questions for Discussion and Further Study

1. Is the thought of the Holy Spirit as a vulnerable expression of God's presence new to you? How does this impact your perspective on masculine vulnerability?

2. Do you believe you are owned by God? Why or why not? If not, what's preventing you?

3. Read Ephesians 2. In this passage Paul addresses all three stages of empowered manhood. Identify for yourself where Paul alludes to being known by God, grown by God, and owned by God.

4. What do you hope God will empower you to accomplish for his kingdom's purposes?

5. What's the difference between being an admirer of Jesus and being a follower of Jesus?

Visit empoweredmanhood.thinkific.com for more insights and resources about being owned by God.

NOTES

CHAPTER 6

EMPOWERED BY THE LIGHT

His divine power has given us everything we need for a
godly life through our knowledge of him who called us
by his own glory and goodness.

—2 Peter 1:3

The Interplay of the 3 Stages of Empowered Manhood

Let's review the journey to empowered manhood that we've been
on. First, the empowered man is Known by God, where he experiences a new, secure identity as a beloved son of God. Then, as a
man entrusts himself to Jesus, he is Grown by God—not by virtue
of his own discipline or willpower, but by virtue of God working in
him. Finally, a man is Owned by God when the Holy Spirit empowers him to transcend his own selfish agenda so that he can accomplish God's redemptive purposes.

As I mentioned in chapter 2, these three stages are a framework for helping us understand God's work in our lives. They are
not prescriptive or formulaic. These stages do not always play out
in sequential order; however, they often have a rhythm. There is

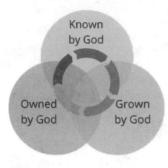

interplay between the three stages as the Holy Spirit, "blows wherever it pleases" (John 3:8).

For example, even after years of the Holy Spirit working in my life, I have to continually return to the foundational truth of my identity in Christ and remind myself that I am known by God. Once I find that security again, God grows me in new ways, which inevitably leads me to a new understanding of how and where he's going to utilize me for his purposes.

In this chapter I will use various examples to elaborate on the interplay between the three stages of empowered manhood and how they materialize in our experience. God is active in every one of our lives in different ways; these examples are meant to give you a better perspective so that you will more easily recognize when and how he is moving in your life specifically.

Stepping into the Light

John's hand was shaky and clammy when I took hold of it and pulled him in for a "bro hug." As a pastor in a church with around two thousand in attendance every weekend, I greet a lot of people in the lobby, and see a lot of people who haven't been in church for a while. On this specific day, though, I had a very unique opportunity to see John in the lobby for the first time. John and I had met previously for lunch, but this was the first time he had stepped foot in a church in a long time.

The first time I saw him he was standing next to one of the pillars in our lobby, sheepishly trying to get my attention but acting as if he didn't want anyone to find out he was there. It was like one of those spy movies where the main characters are conspicuously walking around a party communicating to each other through ear-pieces and trying not to be found out. John was hyper-alert. As I approached him to enthusiastically say hi, I couldn't believe it. He was literally shaking.

Later I found out that John had the fear of God in him on mul-tiple levels. It took all the courage he had just to walk through the doors of the church that day. He came trembling into the presence of God. John knew he was sinful, and he wasn't convinced that God wouldn't strike him down right there in the lobby. On top of that, John also had a touch of social anxiety that normally prevented him from going into crowded places like church. So, he had two big obstacles to overcome in attending church that day for the first time in a long time. John was timidly stepping out of the darkness and into the light, where he would be known by God.

Our conversation was brief but positive. God spoke poignantly to John that day through the message and he was emotional. He ducked out quickly, and I'm sure he spent most of the rest of the day thinking about the implications of what had just transpired.

He and I met again for lunch to debrief, and he shared more of his story with me as he slowly became more comfortable with the revealing nature of the light of the gospel. Eventually John dis-covered what I had learned years earlier—that God's mercy and grace and loving embrace awaits in the light—not judgment or condemnation.

It was a recent breakup that had shed light into John's life and made him aware of his sin and brokenness. He had always known that God was there and he had remembered, like the prodigal son (Luke 15:11–32), that he was probably better off returning home even if he would be sacrificing the status of sonship to become a slave in his father's house. However, if you know the parable, you know the son did not end up being his father's slave.

The story picks up in Luke 15:20: "So he got up and went to his father. But while he was still a long way off, his father saw him and was filled with compassion for him; he ran to his son, threw his arms around him and kissed him." This is what John experienced as he stepped back into the church, back into the light, and back into relationship with his heavenly Father. Through myself, other pastors, and the rest of the church community, John experienced the love of the Father he had been missing for so long. He realized he was known by God and discovered the privileged status of being God's beloved son for the first time.

Then John was drawn into fellowship with other believers in the church through Bible studies, men's groups, and social activities where he was grown by God. He was no longer nervous about being in the lobby but instead became quite the social butterfly, moving from person to person, enjoying the love of the Father through everyone he got to know.

Eventually, after John had grown a bit, he started living like he was owned by God. He stopped compromising his faith in his search for a wife and soon met a woman who was also a Christian. They married after insisting on living separately, remaining chaste. He started looking at his job differently and became intentional about how he lived out his faith among his coworkers. He started to see his work as a way to serve the Lord, rather than just his bosses. After all, he was now owned by God, and wherever he went he wasn't just concerned with his own priorities. He now prioritized his Father's business.

Forced into the Light

Eric had been unfaithful, and when he and his wife walked up to me in the lobby the wear and tear of their experience was weighing heavy on them. Not knowing the specifics of their situation, I told them about the hope God could provide, even in their complicated and sordid past. They were overwhelmed emotionally because they hadn't heard that before, and it was a lifeline to them in their desperate situation. I also think that God spoke through me in that moment, to assure them that he knew them.

Eric and I had the opportunity to meet weekly for almost a year, and I had the privilege of watching God's light penetrate his heart and transform him from the inside out. It took very intentional times of meeting and digging into Scripture for Eric to be grown by God. Often, during our times together, he explained that even though he had previously taught adult Sunday school, he felt he was seeing and understanding Scripture for the first time. The truth was that, even though he knew a lot about God and the Bible, he hadn't studied Scripture within the context of being known by God. Everything changes when you're learning about the God who knows you. He was finally forced into sitting in the chair, putting his full weight on it, and experiencing the rest Jesus offers in relationship with him.

Eric used to be an elder in his church and an active parishioner in the community. Most people knew him and his family, so when his sin was suddenly revealed it had ripples that were far-reaching. Eric's sin impacted everyone around him, from other elders and parishioners in his church to their neighbors, to their kids. Sadly, our sin can have painful consequences.

He admitted to me later that what made matters worse was how prideful and dogmatic he'd been about his faith previously. This bred even more anger and hostility about the hypocrisy of his sin from those who were closest to him. The danger here is that the consequences of our sin can push us back toward the dark, because those consequences can seem unbearable. The dark is more comfortable in times like these, and it's easy to fall for its lies all over again. This is where connection with other men is so important, especially when God has us in the fire of the forge.

I found out later that before he and I met, Eric had isolated himself from everyone he knew because the shame was too great. He found himself sitting in his house alone, preparing to take his own life. Fortunately, he couldn't find everything he felt was necessary to carry out his plan, so he put it off. Shortly after that incident was when he and his wife met me in the lobby.

As we met over that year, it was amazing to watch God's Spirit move in Eric in profound ways. He went from being a prideful and dogmatic Pharisee to becoming a softened, empathetic place of refuge for other men who struggled in similar ways.

God owns Eric today. He and his wife have a stronger marriage than when they started. He is meeting with many men on a regular basis, leading recovery groups, and helping men step out of the dark and into the light where they can be known by God the way he's now known by God. Now, Eric gets to be part of God's plan in growing these other men and moving *them* from being self-reliant to being owned by God. Before God got a hold of Eric and grew him, he wouldn't have come close to the men he now spends most of his time with.

The Rest of My Story

The couple of weeks after Lisa walked in on me while I was on the computer looking at porn were the hardest weeks of our young lives. Just about everyone we knew who was close to us found out about the sin I was hiding in the dark. In a sense, my worst nightmare had been realized. And yet, it wasn't as bad as I thought it was going to be. In fact, I was surprised by the grace and unconditional love that God lavished on us.

Other men came to my side to support and encourage me. Other couples, young and old, stood with us and reassured us that we weren't alone. Women came alongside Lisa, spending time with her in Scripture, and giving her the strength to forgive me and to remain committed to our marriage.

I experienced my own version of God's loving embrace through a CLC men's discipleship group. CLC, or Christ-Led Communities, is a men's discipleship ministry with a focus on cultivating deep, lasting relationships among men. The curriculum was great, but it was seeing the transparency of the other men in the group that convinced me that I was in a safe place. I was able to share the things I had been hiding for so long without the fear of being judged or abandoned. The men in the group responded positively with encouragement and love. I was known by God through these other men who also had the Holy Spirit in their lives. And by his Holy Spirit God was making himself known to me through these other men.

In his book *Cry Like a Man*, Jason Wilson says it well, "Every boy needs a crew; every man needs camaraderie and a safe space to not only express his emotions but also to release them, venting his cares to someone who cares. . . . As men, we must take care of ourselves by truthfully expressing ourselves with other men we can trust. No matter our age, transparency will set us free."[8] The light of the gospel shining into our lives is always an invitation toward transparency. This light is coming from God's exit door which leads to freedom, joy, and peace.

It was the first time in my life where I was able to be completely honest and open with a group of other men without the fear of shame or retribution. Every time I confessed what I had been hiding in the dark I experienced God's grace afresh and he grew me through it, just like he promises in 1 John 1:7: "But if we walk in the light, as he is in the light, we have fellowship with one another, and the blood of Jesus, his Son, purifies us from all sin."

In CLC, we like to explain the relational aspect of discipleship through "the four Ts"—Time, Trust, Transparency, and Transformation. Men need to spend Time together, which builds Trust. Trust leads to Transparency, and Transparency brings Transformation. This is exactly what happened to me. Within that community of men, my band of brothers, transformation happened almost without effort. There was a strength I gained from those men that enabled me to live intentionally like I never had before. I began making decisions that were clearly motivated by the Spirit at work within me rather than the lies of the dark. I was now owned by God.

Now, I see the light as my safe place and refuge, not as the threat I felt before. I know God will meet me there with mercy and grace. The dark has become as scary as my grandparents' cellar once again and I avoid it at all costs. So, whenever I meet with a new guy, I always try to fit in my story of redemption because I am compelled. This is only through the work of the Holy Spirit because before then, I was obsessed with how people viewed me. I needed to impress and gain their approval, even if it meant lying. Now I am owned by God, and my will has succumbed to his. This transparency has opened countless doors of connection with other men who, through my sharing, found strength to share their own struggle. The Holy Spirit uses these interactions to grow me and the men I meet with.

It is still hard and painful sometimes to be confronted with my sin, especially as a man. I want so desperately to arrive, to be finished, and to experience resolution. But if I am humbly willing to accept it, knowing that I am secure and known by God, it has the power to transform me. Then, as God grows me, he shows me where or how he wants to use me as a result of that new work in my life. Nothing is wasted.

Our default, as men, is often to fight against this process. Our egos are fragile, and we don't want to be reminded of our sin and dependency on God. This is the struggle the apostle Paul describes in Romans 7:15–20: "For I have the desire to do what is good, but I cannot carry it out" (v. 18). If you're married, you know what I'm talking about. The longer I'm married, the more I realize that marriage is one of God's primary tools to break us down and humble us. British American poet W. H. Auden said it best: "We would rather be ruined than changed. We would rather die in our dread than climb the cross of the present and let our illusions die." This was true for the disempowered Mike. I was enslaved by my illusions because I thought that was where I found security. The empowered Mike has been humbled by the utter destruction of my illusions. Yet out of the ashes rose a whole new identity in Christ that proved infinitely more secure.

Empowered by the Light of the Gospel

Finally, I understood what other Christians described as "peace," "rest," and "joy." Before this I was still circling the chair of faith, hesitant to put my full weight on it. Those words seemed so foreign to my Christian experience before God brought me into the light and caused me to sit and find rest. And because I did, the truth of Jesus's words in Matthew 11:28–30 ring refreshingly true: "Come to me, all you who are weary and burdened, and I will give you rest. Take my yoke upon you and learn from me, for I am gentle and humble in heart, and you will find rest for your souls. For my yoke is easy and my burden is light."

That was exactly how I felt, weary and burdened. Somehow, I had been convinced, like most men, that it was up to me. I was on my own. There was some ambiguous standard I was required to live up to, or achieve, in order to be acceptable to God and others. And so I labored for success and approval and status. However, these things proved elusive and never ultimately satisfied. Being *known by God* was the only thing that brought me true rest.

Once I was seated in that chair, and fully trusted Jesus, I was able to feel the strength and reliability of God's faithfulness. The longer I was in the chair the more confident I became in God's goodness. The truth of the gospel was solidified in my heart, and eventually my actions became motivated by that truth, rather than my futile attempts at moral excellence, or performance, or significance. God had already proved his love and commitment to me, so I had nothing to fear. This gave me the courage to do hard things like embrace conflict, confess sin, and share my feelings with my wife.

One of my favorite psalms uses extraordinary language to describe the "empowered man":

> Even in darkness light dawns for the upright, for those who are *gracious* and *compassionate* and *righteous*. . . .
>
> Surely the righteous will *never be shaken*; they will be *remembered forever*.
>
> They will have *no fear* of bad news; their hearts are *steadfast*, trusting in the LORD.
>
> Their hearts are *secure*, they will have *no fear*; in the end they will look in *triumph* on their foes.
> (Psalm 112:4, 6–8)

What man wouldn't want to be known as triumphant, fearless, steadfast, never shaken, or remembered forever—in addition to being gracious, compassionate, and righteous? This is a man I want to know. This is a man I want to spend time with. This is a man I want to be!

Remember, none of this comes about because we work hard to achieve it or muster the willpower to scale the mountain of "self-help." In fact, the word "righteous" that you see in the passage above does not indicate that there is a righteousness in the person themself. Everywhere you see the word "righteous" in the Bible describing a person, you can replace that word with "miserable, wretched, helpless, evil sinner, who found refuge from judgment under the shelter of Jesus."

When the word "righteous" is used to describe someone, it simply means that that person has placed their trust in God. They are sitting on the chair, in dependence on God's provision. Therefore, God has declared them righteous because of their dependence on him, not based on their own merit (see Romans 8:3; 9:16; Ephesians 2:8–9). This is very freeing because our ultimate standing before God is not dependent on us, but on the rock-solid commitment of God's unconditional love. We can be bold and courageous because the outcome depends on God, not us. It is *God* who grows us.

Suddenly I have an abundance of grace and love to offer others because I have been forgiven and loved lavishly by God. I don't need to hang on to my anger or allow bitterness to weigh me down because Jesus paid the penalty—not only for my sin, but for every sin committed against me. Justice has been served and I can trust that God will handle the guilty. It doesn't mean that I still don't experience pain and suffering from sinful treatment at the hands of others. Trust me, it still hurts, but when I remember how gracious

God has been to me, I lose the desire to seek retribution for the suffering I experience as a consequence of someone else's sin. Overall, this produces abundant joy and peace. I'm not angry or bitter anymore. I have an advocate in Jesus, the ultimate judge who will righteously judge the whole world.

I am also not confined to the expectation of a positive outcome in this life, because God's redemptive plan for humanity transcends the duration of my life. When Psalm 112 says the empowered man "will be remembered forever" (v. 6) or that "he will look in triumph on his foes" (v. 8), we must broaden our perspective and not simply apply it to our fragile and finite lives. No man will be remembered forever who is not already known by God—in which case, he will remember us for eternity.

As we're grown by God, we begin to understand that our "foes" are not just the people who think ill of us but anyone who opposes God's kingdom purposes. Therefore, we're victorious when God is victorious. I don't need to be wealthy, healthy, or successful by the world's standards. God simply calls me to be faithful to him. When I do that, I trust that his kingdom purposes will be achieved, even if that means I am just an "extra" in his drama. After all, the story of human history is *his*-story, not mine. I could never operate this way under my own power, otherwise I would want it to be all about me. This attitude came from being *owned by God*.

Most certainly there have been times of great struggle, falling back into unhealthy patterns of thought and behavior, and being deceived by the disempowering lies of the dark again. These have been painful reminders that I need to relinquish control again and loosen my grip. As a man who has struggled myself in the dark and found empowerment, I can say with confidence that it doesn't take much for God to work a miracle in your life. Simply acknowledge your need and choose to turn toward the light of his truth. God has done everything, and he calls us into his light to experience the fruit of the finished work of Christ. This is where we will experience manhood empowered by the light of the gospel.

Chapter Summary

- The four stages of manhood—known by God, grown by God, owned by God, and empowered by God—are not meant to be formulaic or prescriptive. Rather, they provide a framework for helping men understand God's work in their lives.

- John is a great example of a man deciding to step into the light as a result of Holy Spirit's work in his life. Through church and relationships with other believers, the gospel lit his way out of the dark and guided him into the light of the truth, where he discovered a new confidence in God.

- Eric had been walking around the chair of faith, encouraging everyone else to sit but never finding rest himself. It wasn't until his sin was dragged into the light that he was forced to trust God and found true rest, joy, and purpose.

- After years of living out of fear and insecurity, I found confidence in Christ—but only after everything I was hiding had been exposed. Being laid bare, yet experiencing God's unconditional love, set me free to humbly walk in the light as He is in the light, in order to be a light for the glory of God.

Questions for Discussion and Further Study

1. Which story from the examples in this chapter resonated most with you and your experience? Explain.

2. Have you stepped into the light, or were you forced into the light? Does it make a difference? Why or why not?

3. Read John 15. What elements of being known by God, grown by God, and owned by God do you see in that chapter?

4. Describe what the interplay between the three stages of empowered manhood looks like in your own life.

5. Read Psalm 111, which describes God; and Psalm 112, which describes an empowered man. These two psalms were written for the purpose of being read together. Discuss how these two psalms relate to each other. How does God's character, described in Psalm 111, translate to who the man of God is in Psalm 112?

Visit empoweredmanhood.thinkific.com for more insights and resources about being owned by God.

NOTES

EPILOGUE

By now, more than anything, I pray that you are convinced of God's unimaginable greatness. I hope that God has become so much bigger to you and that you see him as being completely sufficient. If that's true for you, then most likely you have been empowered, and that's what our families need—men empowered by the light of the gospel.

However, you must remain in Jesus, as He remains in you (John 15:4). Apart from him, you can do nothing (John 15:5). You are desperately dependent on God and you always will be. In spite of what many people think, even after we die and enter into eternity, we will still be dependent on God. The idea that we'll be perfect and know everything once we arrive in heaven is not true. From the very beginning, when Adam and Eve were created in the garden, humanity was designed to be dependent on God and to grow in our knowledge of him for all eternity. We'll still make mistakes; we'll still have to learn how to master skills; there will still be misunderstanding. The big difference is that, in heaven, sin won't hinder us anymore.

Therefore, as we're known by God, grown by God, and owned by God, it's important to remember that this is all in preparation for the eternal life to come: "For physical training is of some value, but godliness has value for all things, holding promise for both the present life *and the life to come*" (1 Timothy 4:8, emphasis added).

We're currently being trained by the Holy Spirit for the life to come, and nothing is wasted! Not even your sin and failures.

As *Maximized Manhood* author Edwin Louis Cole puts it, "Maturity doesn't come with age but begins with the acceptance of responsibility. The first Adam in the Garden of Eden refused to accept responsibility for his actions, while the Last Adam, the Lord Jesus Christ, accepted responsibility for the actions of the entire world."[9] As we step into the light to accept responsibility for our sin, we're met by Jesus—the only man of true power, who already accepted responsibility on our behalf by dying on the cross and rising from the dead. Take comfort in this! The fact that you've made it through this book means that Jesus has most likely already been at work in and around you. Don't take that for granted; rather, use this profound truth to motivate yourself to trust him in your next step.

The next thing you should do, if you haven't already, is to go be in the presence of God—including through his other children, where he can begin reassuring you that you are known by God. Start connecting with other men who are serious about growing in their faith and you will be amazed at how you will be grown by God. Then, entrust yourself to God for his purposes and expect him to use you in powerful ways as someone who is owned by God.

We need each other, men. The empowered man is connected to the power source of the Holy Spirit through church community, a brotherhood of men, and the Bible. When you unplug from these, you are disempowered and at risk of getting lost in the dark again. We need brothers and sisters in Christ, who are also living in the light, to remind us of the truth so that we can make the proper course corrections when needed.

I remember when I played high school football and all of the skill players would take turns running through the gauntlet with the football. The gauntlet was a large metal frame with protruding,

padded arms attached to springs. Running through those arms sim-
ulated running through defensive players who were trying to tackle
you. It wasn't uncommon to get bruised as those arms swung back
and forth, especially if you were following someone else through.
The point was to get used to contact and train yourself to hold the
football tight so that you wouldn't fumble. Think of relationships as
the gauntlet for sanctification. "Sanctification" is simply a theologi-
cal word to describe the process of growing in our faith.

Relationships are the primary means by which God grows us,
because it's where the rubber meets the road with regard to obedience. It's easy to give mental assent to God's goodness when we're
isolated from relationships. It doesn't cost us anything. It's in the
context of relationship, where we have more to lose, that we discover whether we really trust God. For example, will we trust God
enough to overlook an offense? Will we respond with grace when
someone treats us poorly? When we sin, will we confess it? Will we
be humble enough to ask for forgiveness? Will we love our enemies,
or will we seek revenge? Will we be generous to those who don't
appreciate it? This is why Jesus said that the greatest commandment
is, "'Love the Lord your God with all your heart and with all your
soul and with all your mind.' And the second is like it: 'Love your
neighbor as yourself.' All the Law and the Prophets hang on these
two commandments" (Matthew 22:37–40).

When Jesus says that the "Law and the Prophets hang on these
two commandments," he's saying that the entire Bible to that point
(they didn't have the New Testament yet) can be summed up as
obedience to these two commands, which involve relationship with
God and relationship with others. There's no getting around it—we
must be in relationship to grow in our faith.

With that in mind, I want to encourage you to join the Empowered Manhood Facebook group, where you can start making

connections and find empowered men near you. The point of the group is to connect with other like-minded men in person, not just to interact online where there is little cost to relationship. Don't let this Facebook group, or any virtual group for that matter, replace meeting with men in person and doing life together. As I said earlier, go to church where you can start building your own band of brothers or join someone else's.

Remember, the journey continues at empoweredmanhood. thinkific.com. You'll find a growing library of resources to help you along in your specific situation. Maybe you need to be reminded or convinced of the fact that you are known by God. You might need help figuring out how to put yourself in a position to be grown by God. Or you could be at a point where you're looking for a specific opportunity that reflects the truth that you are owned by God. Whatever it is, I have designed additional digital courses to help you think through what that looks like for you. It would be my privilege to play a role in your story of redemption and sanctification.

All right men, it's time to get out there. Let's humbly walk in the light together, as Jesus is in the light, in order to be lights for the glory of God. Let's live empowered by the light of the gospel!

ABOUT THE AUTHOR

As a recovering pornography addict with twenty years of experience discipling men, Mike Hatch is all too familiar with the struggles men face. Since discovering empowered manhood himself, Mike's life mission has been *to humbly walk in the light, as Jesus is in the light, in order to be a light for the glory of God* (1 John 1:7).

Currently Mike fulfills this mission as the National Relationship Generator for CLC (Christ Led Communities), where he consults with churches and ministry leaders about men's discipleship. He also hosts CLC's Empowered Manhood Podcast.

A graduate of Trinity Evangelical Divinity School, Mike started his ministry career in Young Life before becoming the men's pastor at a large church in Pittsburgh, PA. Mike lives in Pittsburgh with his beautiful bride and amazing teenage son.

ENDNOTES

Introduction

1. Chase Replogle, *The 5 Masculine Instincts* (Chicago, IL: Moody Publishers, 2022), 88.

Chapter 1—Disempowered

2. Scott Neuffer, "Dark & Light Symbolism in Literature" penandthepad.com, August 6, 2022, https://penandthepad.com/dark-light-symbolism-literature-2137.html.

3. Jeremy Stolow and Birgit Meyer, "Enlightening Religion: Light and Darkness in Religious Knowledge about Religion," The Center for Critical Research and Religion, May 8, 2021, https://journals.sagepub.com/doi/full/10.1177/20503032211015276.

4. C. J. Forceville and T. Renckens. "The 'Good Is Light' and 'Bad Is Dark' Metaphor in Feature Films," *Metaphor and the Social World*, 2013 3(2), 160–179, https://pure.uva.nl/ws/files/2026902/136782_LIGHT_DARK_in_feature_film_revised_version_June_2013_distr._version.pdf.

5. J. S. Shelton, *Umuzzled* (self-published, J. S. Shelton, 2019), 26.

6. Gary Haugen, *Just Courage* (Downers Grove, IL: InterVarsity Press, 2008), 17.

Chapter 5—Stage 3: Owned by God

7. Edwin Louis Cole, *Maximized Manhood* (New Kensington, PA: Whitaker House, 1982, 2001) 106.

Chapter 6—Empowered by the Light

8.   Jason Wilson, *Cry Like a Man* (Colorado Springs, CO: David C Cook, 2019) 93.

Epilogue

9.   Cole, *Maximized Manhood*, 163.

SHE'S UP TO NO GOOD

ALSO BY
SARA GOODMAN CONFINO

For the Love of Friends